Science Projects About
the Physics of Sports

Science Projects About
the Physics of Sports

Robert Gardner

Science Projects

Enslow Publishers, Inc.

40 Industrial Road	PO Box 38
Box 398	Aldershot
Berkeley Heights, NJ 07922	Hants GU12 6BP
USA	UK

http://www.enslow.com

Library of Congress Cataloging-in-Publication Data

Gardner, Robert, 1929–
    Science projects about the physics of sports / by Robert Gardner.
      p. cm. — (Science projects)
    Includes bibliographical references and index.
    Summary: Presents science projects and experiments related to sports, covering such
topics as speed, Newton's Laws, force and motion, gravity, friction, and collisions.
    ISBN 0-7660-1167-4
    1. Force and energy—Experiments Juvenile literature. 2. Motion—Experiments
Juvenile literature. 3. Sports—Experiments Juvenile literature. 4. Science projects
Juvenile literature. [1. Sports—Experiments. 2. Force and energy—Experiments.
3. Motion—Experiments. 4. Experiments. 5. Science projects.] I. Title. II. Series:
Gardner, Robert, 1929– Science projects.
QC73.4.G375   2000
530'.078—dc21   99-34119
                                               CIP

Printed in the United States of America

10 9 8 7 6 5 4 3 2 1

To Our Readers:
All Internet addresses in this book were active and appropriate when we went to press. Any
comments or suggestions can be sent by e-mail to Comments@enslow.com or to the address
on the back cover.

Illustration Credits: Stephen F. Delisle

Cover Illustration: Jerry McCrea (foreground); © Corel Corporation (background).

AUG - - 2000

Contents

*appropriate ideas for science fair project

*appropriate ideas for science fair project

Introduction

While enjoying sports, you can learn about science. This book is filled with projects and experiments related to sports. Most of the materials you will need to carry out these activities involve sports equipment and athletic fields or courts. For some of the experiments, you will need one or more people to help you. It would be best if you work with friends or adults who enjoy experimenting as much as you do. In that way, you will all enjoy the experiment. **If any risk of injury is involved in an experiment, it will be made known to you. In some cases, to avoid any danger to you, you will be asked to work with an adult. Please do so.** We do not want you to take any chances that could lead to an injury. It is a good idea to warm up and stretch your muscles before performing sports. You have probably seen professional athletes doing so before they go into games. Your school coaches can suggest some routines, or you can check sports books in the library.

Like other good scientists, you will find it useful to record your ideas, notes, data, and any conclusions you draw from your experiments in a notebook. By so doing, you can keep track of the information you gather and the conclusions you reach. Record keeping will allow you to refer to experiments you have done that may help you in doing other projects in the future. In some of the experiments, you will have to make some calculations. Therefore, you may find it helpful to have a calculator nearby as you do these experiments and analyze the data you collect.

Science Fairs

Some of the projects in this book may be appropriate for a science fair. Those projects are indicated with an asterisk (*). However, judges at such fairs do not reward projects or experiments that are simply copied from books. For example, plugging numbers into a formula you do not understand will not impress judges. A graph of data collected from experiments you have done that is used to find a relationship between two variables would be more likely to receive serious consideration.

Science fair judges tend to reward creative thought and imagination. It is difficult to be creative or imaginative unless you are really interested in your project; consequently, be sure to choose a subject that appeals to you. And before you jump into a project, consider your own talents and the cost of materials you will need.

If you decide to use a project found in this book for a science fair, you should find ways to modify or extend it. This should not be difficult because you will probably discover that as you do these projects, new ideas for experiments will come to mind—experiments that could make excellent science fair projects, particularly because the ideas are your own and are interesting to you.

If you decide to enter a science fair and have never done so before, you should read some of the books listed in the "Further Reading" section, such as *Science Fair Projects—Planning, Presenting, Succeeding*, which is one of the other books in this series. These books deal specifically with science fairs and will provide plenty of helpful hints and lots of useful information that will enable you to avoid the pitfalls that sometimes plague first-time entrants. You will learn how to prepare appealing reports that include charts and graphs, how to set up and display your work, how to present your project, and how to relate to judges and visitors.

Safety First

Most of the projects included in this book are perfectly safe. However, the following safety rules are well worth reading before you start any project.

1. Do any experiments or projects, whether from this book or of your own design, under the supervision of a science teacher or other knowledgeable adult.

2. Read all instructions carefully before proceeding with a project. If you have questions, check with your supervisor before going any further.

3. Maintain a serious attitude while conducting experiments. Fooling around can be dangerous to you and to others.

4. Wear approved safety goggles when you are working with a flame or doing anything that might cause injury to your eyes.

5. Do not eat or drink while experimenting.

6. Do not go on a frozen lake or pond without permission from an adult.

7. Have a first-aid kit nearby while you are experimenting.

8. Do not put your fingers or any object, other than properly designed electrical connectors, into electrical outlets.

9. Never experiment with household electricity except under the supervision of a knowledgeable adult.

10. Do not touch a lit high-wattage bulb. Lightbulbs produce light, but they also produce heat.

11. Many substances are poisonous. Do not taste any unless instructed to do so.

12. If a thermometer breaks, inform your adult supervisor. Do not touch either the mercury or the broken glass with your bare hands.

13. Wear appropriate protective gear, such as helmets and leg guards, for all sports activities in the projects you do.

1

Speed, Sports, and Science

What is one of the basic qualities that scouts for professional teams look for in young players? The answer is speed!

Speed is the distance that something moves divided by the time it takes to move that distance. Speed can be represented mathematically by a simple formula:

$$\text{speed} = \text{distance} \div \text{time, or speed} = \frac{\text{distance}}{\text{time}}, \text{ or } s = \frac{d}{t}.$$

You may think that speed and velocity mean the same thing; that is, distance divided by time. But there is a difference. Velocity is speed in a particular direction. If someone tells you a sprinter runs 10 meters in 10 seconds, you know the runner's speed is 1.0 m/s. But if she tells you a sailboat is traveling 1.0 m/s northwest, you know the boat's velocity. She has told you not only the boat's speed but also the direction in which it is traveling. To boaters, hikers, and bikers, it is more important to know velocity than speed. If you are traveling at the right speed but in the wrong direction, you will never reach your destination.

1-1*
Speed on the Base Paths

Covering ground as a fielder, stealing bases, and running the bases quickly is often the difference between winning or losing in baseball. Can a base runner round the bases at the same speed as a sprinter in track? You can find out by doing an experiment.

Things you will need:

- baseball field
- stopwatch or watch with a second hand or mode
- notebook
- pen or pencil
- tape measure
- friend

Find a baseball field and do some warm-up and stretching exercises. Then stand on home plate. Have a friend shout, "Go!" as he or she starts a stopwatch or notes the time on a watch with a second hand or mode. When you hear "Go," run around the bases as fast as you can. Be sure to touch each base. Have your friend record the number of seconds it took you to round the bases.

The distance between bases is 90 feet. (On a Little League or softball field it is only 60 feet.) What is the total distance from home plate to first base, then to second and third base, and finally back to home plate? Is that the actual distance a player runs after hitting an inside-the-park homer?

Now walk at an even pace between home plate and first base. Count the number of steps you take. Then move to the outfield. Use the same even pace to mark off a distance that is four times as long as the distance from home to first base. For example, if you walked 100 steps between home and first, measure off a distance that is 400 steps long in the outfield. This distance should be very close to 360 feet, the same as the distance of the base paths.

Have your friend measure the time it takes you to run this distance. How does the time to run the straight-line distance (360 ft) in the outfield compare with the time it took you to run around the base paths in the infield? Based on the results of your experiment,

12

can a base runner in baseball run as fast as a sprinter in track? If not, why not?

Exploring on Your Own

Because you round the bases, you run farther than 360 feet when you hit an inside-the-park homer. Run the bases as if you had hit an inside-the-park homer on a field that has dirt base paths so you can see your footprints while someone times you with a stopwatch. Use a tape measure to determine the actual distance you traveled. What was your speed? How does it compare with your speed along a straight-line path of the same length? In addition to distance traveled, what else affects your speed in running the bases?

James "Cool Papa" Bell, who played in the Negro Leagues before baseball was integrated in 1947, could round the bases in 13 seconds. Compare Bell's speed on the base paths with modern players. You can do this with a stopwatch at a game or on television. You do not have to wait for an inside-the-park homer; you can time doubles or triples and calculate the answer, considering the difference in distance.

Compare Bell's speed on the base paths with the speed of modern sprinters who run 100 or 200 meter races. Explain why Bell's speed was slower, even though he might have won a race against these present-day sprinters.

1-2*
Speed on Ice

Speed on skates is essential if you want to play hockey. But you must also be able to turn, change direction quickly, and skate backward. If you did Experiment 1-1, you know how fast you can run. Do you think you can skate faster than you can run? You can determine your ice speed by doing this experiment.

To do this experiment you will need a hockey rink or a frozen pond or lake that is safe to skate on. **Check with an adult before you go onto a frozen pond or lake! It may not be safe.**

Things you will need:

- ice skates
- stopwatch or watch with a second hand or mode
- hockey rink, or smooth, frozen pond or lake
- hockey goals or suitable substitutes
- tape measure
- an adult if using outdoor ice
- friend
- notebook
- pen or pencil

After warm-ups and stretching, stand on skates on one side of a hockey goal or a stick that represents a goal. Have a friend with a stopwatch or watch shout, "Go!" and begin timing. When you hear "Go," skate to the opposite goal, go around it, return to the goal from which you started and go around it. Repeat this path twice.

Have your friend record the time it took for you to skate around both goals twice.

With a tape measure, find the distance you skated. Do not forget to include the distance around the goals.

Now, divide the distance you skated, in meters or feet, by the time it took in seconds. This will give you your average speed in meters per second (m/s) or feet per second (f/s). How fast did you skate? How can you convert your skating speed in m/s or ft/s to kilometers per hour (kph) or miles per hour (mph)?

If you repeat the experiment, but skate around the goals five times instead of two, do you think your speed will be faster, slower, or the same? Try it! Were you right?

If possible, find a length of ice that will allow you to skate the same total distance without having to turn. Do you think your speed will be faster, slower, or the same under this condition? Why? Try it! Were you right?

Exploring on Your Own

At the 1994 Olympics, speed skater Aleksandr Golubev of Russia won the 500-meter race in a time of 36.33 seconds. What was his speed in m/s? What was his speed in kph? In mph? How does his speed on skates compare with yours?

Use an almanac to find the winning speed of Olympic runners who ran the 500-meter race. How do their running speeds compare with Olympic skating speeds? Predict and then compare Olympic swimming speeds with running speeds.

1-3
Throwing Speed from the Outfield

Things you will need:

- baseball field
- stopwatch or watch with a second hand or mode
- baseball
- baseball glove
- 2 friends
- notebook
- pen or pencil

A good outfielder must be able to make fast and accurate throws to keep runners from taking an extra base or scoring. His or her throws must get back to the infield or home plate as quickly as possible. One of the most common mistakes among young players is the way they throw the ball from the outfield. They try to throw the ball to a catcher or baseman so that it is in the air when it reaches their teammate. In this experiment, you will find out why a different kind of throw is better.

Before you begin this experiment, be sure to do some stretching exercises, especially with your throwing arm. Then have a catch with someone to be sure your arm is warmed up. Once you are ready, stand in center field and get ready to make a throw to home plate.

One friend with a stopwatch or a watch with a second hand or mode should stand near home plate. A second friend will stand on home plate and act as your catcher. Your friend with the watch will measure the time it takes the ball to reach home plate after it leaves your hand. He or she will then record that time in a notebook.

Your first throw should be made at an upward angle so that the ball reaches the plate and the catcher in the air without bouncing on the ground. For the second part of the experiment, throw the ball so that its flight is almost horizontal. The ball should take one or two hops before reaching home plate.

Repeat the experiment several times. Then, if possible, have several different people carry out the same experiment.

Which kind of throw takes less time to reach home plate? Should a long throw from an outfielder always reach an infielder in the air, or is it better if it bounces once or twice? Can you explain why?

Should throws to first base made by infielders bounce or travel entirely through the air? Explain your answer.

1-4
Are Passes Really Faster?

Basketball coaches tell players with a fast break opportunity, "Pass the ball, do not dribble it up the court." Soccer coaches tell players, "Pass the ball, don't dribble it up the field." Hockey coaches tell players, "If possible, pass the puck. Don't carry it up the ice on your stick." Are these coaches right? The experiments that follow will help you to find out. You can do all the experiments, or you can choose to do the one connected with the sport you like best.

Things you will need:

- basketball, soccer ball, or two hockey pucks
- hockey sticks
- ice skates
- stopwatch or watch with second hand or mode
- basketball court, soccer field, or hockey rink
- several friends
- notebook
- pen or pencil

Basketball

Do some warm-ups and stretching. Then stand on the end line at one side of a basketball court. Have a friend with a stopwatch stand at midcourt. At the moment your friend shouts "Go!" he or she will start timing. As soon as you hear "Go," dribble the ball as fast as you can toward the other basket. When you reach the midcourt line, your friend will stop the watch or note the time that has elapsed since shouting "Go." He or she will then record the time it took you to dribble the ball half the length of the court.

Now repeat the experiment. But this time, when you hear "Go," throw the ball up the court as hard as you can to a second friend standing at midcourt. Your first friend will note and record the elapsed time at the moment your second friend catches the ball.

Compare the time required to dribble the ball to midcourt with the time required to pass it the same distance. In which case, dribbling or passing, does the ball travel faster? Can you tell from the recorded times how many times faster it traveled?

Design an experiment to measure the average speed of the ball you dribbled and the one you passed. How do the two speeds compare? Do these two speeds agree with the ratio of the speeds you calculated from the two recorded times?

Soccer

After warming up and stretching, stand on the goal line at one end of a soccer field with a soccer ball. Have a friend who is standing at the midfield line with a stopwatch shout "Go!" as he or she starts timing. When you hear "Go," begin dribbling the ball, under control, as fast as you can toward midfield. At the moment you reach midfield, your friend will note and record the elapsed time it took you to dribble the ball half the length of the field.

Stand at the goal line again with a soccer ball. This time, when you hear "Go," kick the ball toward the midfield line, where your partner is standing with the timer. Your friend will note and record the elapsed time when the ball crosses the midfield line.

Compare the time required to dribble the ball to midfield with the time required to pass it the same distance with a good kick. In which case, dribbling or passing, does the ball travel faster? Can you tell from the recorded times how many times faster it traveled?

Design an experiment to measure the average speed of the ball you dribbled and the one you kicked. How do the two speeds compare? Do these two speeds agree with the ratio of the speeds you calculated from the two recorded times?

Hockey

Warm up and stretch. Then stand on skates beside the goal mouth at one end of the rink with your hockey stick and a puck. Have a friend with a stick and puck stand at the blue line at the other side of the red line. Have a second friend shout "Go!" and observe both pucks. When you hear "Go," begin moving your puck forward by carrying it on your stick while skating to the opponent's blue line as fast as you can go. At the same time, upon hearing "Go," your friend will pass a puck toward the goal from which you are starting. Which puck traveled faster, the one you were carrying on your stick or the one your friend passed?

Design an experiment to measure the speed of the puck you carried on your stick and the speed of the one your friend passed. Remember: Speed is distance divided by time.

1-5*
How Fast Can You Shoot a Hockey Puck?

Things you will need:

- stopwatch
- hockey rink
- ice skates
- hockey stick
- hockey puck
- several friends
- tape measure
- notebook
- pen or pencil

To beat a good goalie, a hockey player must be able to shoot the puck at high speed or from close range. How fast can you shoot a puck?

To find out, put a puck on the blue line. Use your stick to shoot the puck with as much force as possible toward the farther end of the rink. At the moment you shoot the puck, have a friend start a stopwatch. He or she should stop the watch when the puck hits the end of the rink, and then record the time. Take several shots and have your friend note and record the time for each one.

Use a tape measure to find the distance between the blue line and the far end of the rink where the puck hit. How can you find the speed at which the puck traveled? How fast did each shot travel? How can you find the average speed of your shots?

Ask several friends or teammates to do the same experiment while you measure the times with the stopwatch. What is the average speed at which each of them shoots the puck?

Exploring on Your Own

Do you think the speed of the puck as it travels down the ice is the same as the speed of the puck when it leaves your stick? Why or why not? Design an experiment to measure the speed of the puck shortly after it leaves your stick. How does the speed of the puck as it leaves your stick compare with its average speed from the blue line to the end of the rink?

1-6
Where to Pass the Puck or Ball

Passing is the fastest way to advance a hockey puck, a football, a soccer ball, or a lacrosse ball. But how do you decide where to pass it? This experiment will help you answer that question.

Suppose you recognize someone entering the far side of a field and proceeding to walk across. You decide that you

Things you will need:
- hockey rink
- hockey puck
- hockey sticks
- friend who skates
- metric ruler
- protractor
- notebook
- pen or pencil

would like to join that person for a walk and some conversation, but you do not want to shout because there are people nearby who are working. To intercept the person, you would walk not directly toward her but along a diagonal path across the field, as shown in Figure 1a. The paths of you and your friend can be represented by vectors (arrows) as shown in Figure 1b. For you to intercept your friend across the field, you must walk faster than she does. The longer arrow in the drawing showing your path demonstrates that you must travel a greater distance than your friend in the same amount of time.

Paths represented by arrows are called displacement vectors (distances in a particular direction). Vectors can also be used to represent velocities (speeds in a particular direction), or any quantity that has magnitude (size) and direction. Vectors can represent accelerations or forces because these quantities have directions as well as magnitudes. Vectors could not be used to represent time or mass because neither time nor mass has a direction. The displacement vectors shown in Figure 1b can be changed to velocity vectors, as shown in Figure 1c. All you need to do is divide the displacement by the time during which it took place. The velocity vectors must

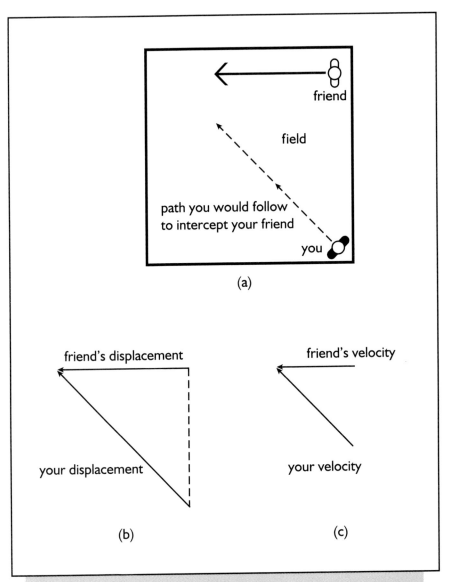

(a)

friend

field

path you would follow
to intercept your friend

you

friend's displacement

your displacement

(b)

friend's velocity

your velocity

(c)

Figure 1. a) To intercept a friend walking in the direction shown, you will have to walk diagonally across the field. b) The paths of you and your friend can be represented by displacement vectors (arrows). These vectors give both the direction and length of the paths. c) If the lengths of the displacement vectors are divided by the time required for the displacement to occur, they become velocity vectors. In this case, how should the two times used as denominators compare?

have the same direction as the displacement vectors, since the two people walked in those directions.

Vectors will help explain how to make passes of the puck in hockey or passes of balls in other sports where passing is part of the game. But only practice will allow you to make judgments about ice or field conditions, teammate speeds, and the many muscular contractions needed to place a puck on the tip of a fast-moving skater's stick or a ball on a receiver's hands, feet, or stick.

Stand near one end of a blue line with your stick and a puck. Have a friend with a stick begin skating up ice from the end of the rink toward the same blue line. As your friend crosses the blue line, send a pass that he or she can receive without changing speed. Of course, you can do a similar experiment in other sports where a ball is used instead of a puck.

To make such a pass, you must take into account the skater's or runner's speed and direction as well as the speed and direction of the puck or ball that you are to pass. The speed of anything combined with its direction is called its velocity.

As you have seen, velocities can be represented by arrows called vectors. The direction of the velocity is given by the head of the arrow. The speed is given by the length of the arrow. In Figure 2a, vector V_s represents the velocity of your skating or running friend moving down the ice or field. Vector V_p represents the speed and direction of the puck or ball you are passing to your friend. It (V_p) must be the vector (not arithmetic) sum of two velocities: (1) a velocity equal to skater's or runner's velocity, V_s, and (2) a velocity, V_x, perpendicular to the skater's or runner's path that will carry the puck to the skater. Figure 2b shows how those two vectors, V_s and V_x, are added (head to tail) to obtain the velocity, V_p, that the puck or ball must have.

$$\mathbf{V}_p = \mathbf{V}_s + \mathbf{V}_x$$

Remember: a vector has both magnitude and direction.

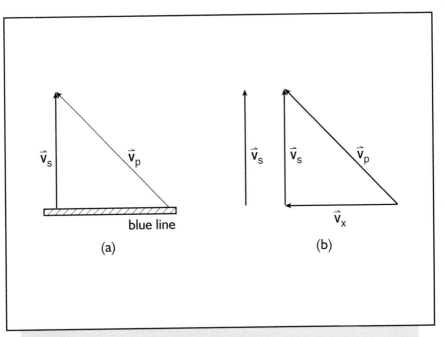

Figure 2. Vectors can represent velocities. In (a), a skater's or runner's speed is represented by the vector $\vec{V}_s$. The velocity of a puck or ball passed to the skater or runner is represented by the vector $\vec{V}_p$. In (b), you can see that $\vec{V}_p$ is the sum of $\vec{V}_s$ and $\vec{V}_x$. $\vec{V}_x$ is the velocity needed to move the puck or ball to the player along a direction perpendicular to his or her path. When $\vec{V}_x$ is added to the player's velocity, $\vec{V}_s$, you obtain $\vec{V}_p$. As you can see, vectors are added head to tail because they have direction as well as magnitude, and their direction is as important as their size.

The scale used in drawing the vectors was 1 cm = 2 m/s. How fast is the skater or runner moving according to the vector diagram? How fast is the puck or ball moving? In what direction must you pass it? Use a protractor to find the direction (angle) relative to the blue line (or field line).

Practice making passes to your friend as he or she skates over the blue line. In what general direction must you pass the puck for your friend to receive it without changing speed? In a game situation, what would cause you to keep the puck rather than passing it?

1-7
How to Kick a Football the Maximum Distance

A football team's punter must know how to make a punt travel different distances. How hard the ball is kicked is one factor. But does the upward angle at which the ball is kicked also make a difference?

To find out, stand on the goal line. You can measure the distance your punts travel by watching to see the yardline on which they hit the ground (not the line to which they may bounce). Try punting a ball with the same force but at different angles to the ground, as shown in Figure 3.

Things you will need:

- football
- football field with lines
- garden hose or a high-powered squirt gun
- cardboard
- protractor
- level surface, such as a stand, garden table, or seesaw support
- friend
- tape measure, meterstick, or yardstick
- marker

Does the angle at which the ball is punted affect the distance it travels? If it does, approximately what angle makes the kick travel farthest? (Do not count any punts that are off the side of your foot or that do not spiral.)

You can determine the angle that produces the longest kick more accurately by doing another experiment. In this experiment, you can control the angle. Use a garden hose or a high-powered squirt gun that uses compressed air. Either device can launch water to represent a football coming off your foot. You can measure the angle at which the water is launched by making a large half-protractor on a sheet of cardboard, as shown in Figure 4.

Place the giant protractor on a level surface. A stand, garden table, or seesaw support will provide a stable and level surface from which to shoot the water. As you know from kicking the football,

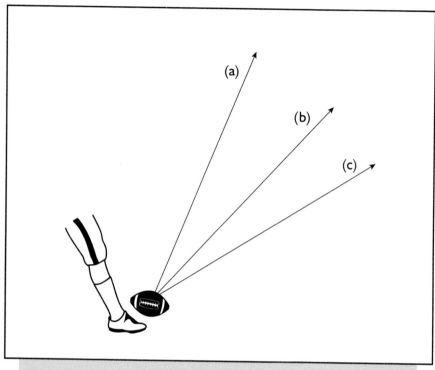

Figure 3. Kick the ball at different upward angles: a) a large upward angle; b) a medium upward angle; c) a small upward angle.

speed, as well as angle, will affect the distance that the water will travel. So you want to be sure the speed at which the water emerges from the squirt gun or hose is the same for each angle at which you fire the water. You can do this by marking the point where the water lands when it is fired horizontally from the level surface. Test several times to be sure that point is approximately the same each time before projecting the water at different angles.

After establishing the fixed range for 0 degrees (level), launch the water at an angle of 10 degrees. Have a partner mark the point where the water lands. The distance from the launch site to the point where the water lands is the range for that angle. It can be measured with a tape measure, a meterstick, or a yardstick. Repeat the experiment

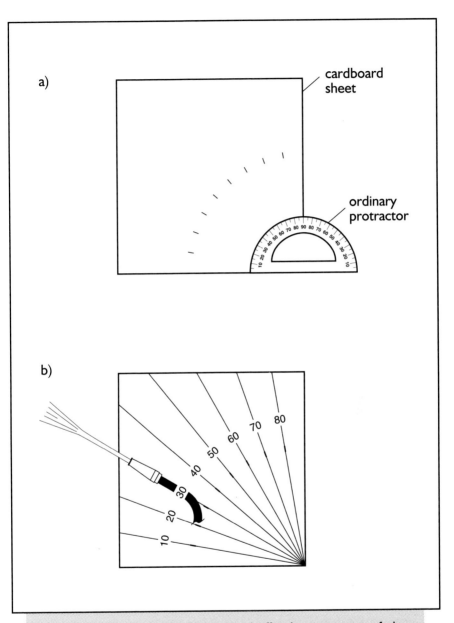

a)

cardboard
sheet

ordinary
protractor

b)

Figure 4. To make a large half-protractor, mark off angles at one corner of a large sheet of cardboard (a). This can be done with a small protractor, as shown. Then use a straight stick or yardstick to extend the lines (b). A hose or large squirt gun can now be used to launch water at known angles.

for 20, 30, 40, 45, 50, 60, 70, 75, and 80 degrees. Why might it be wise to skip 90 degrees?

For which angle is the range greatest? Does this agree with the approximate angle that caused your kicks to travel the farthest? Are there angles for which the range is very nearly or exactly the same? If there are, what are these angles?

1-8*
Speed and Running Surface

Many athletes say they can run faster on some fields than on others. They claim the firmness of the turf affects their speed. This experiment may provide evidence that will support or deny their claims.

Things you will need:

• athletic friend

• sidewalk or lawn

• thick cushions

• stopwatch or watch with second hand or mode

Have a friend who is a good athlete stand on a sidewalk or lawn. Then ask your friend to run in place at what she or he considers a reasonably fast pace. Count the number of steps that your friend takes during a one-minute period while running on this hard surface.

After a five-minute rest, ask your friend to run in place once more at the same pace on a pair of thick cushions instead of the sidewalk or lawn. Again, count the number of steps your friend makes during a one-minute period. What happens to your friend's pace while running on the soft cushions? How do you think a soft field affects a runner's speed? Why do you think it affects his or her speed?

Exploring on Your Own

Design an experiment to find out how running surface affects an athlete's speed. You might compare dry grass, damp grass, Astroturf, cinders, clay, macadam, and so on. On which surface do athletes seem to run fastest? What factors, other than speed, do you think should be considered in choosing the surface for an athletic field?

2

Sports, Forces, and Work

More than three hundred years ago, Sir Isaac Newton published his three laws of motion. Scientific laws are generalizations based on experiments and observations. Newton's laws provide explanations about motion. They are not limited to the motions we see on Earth, but extend to the entire universe. They are truly general and universal.

The first law of motion states that any moving object maintains its velocity (speed and direction) unless a force (a push or a pull) is applied to it. This law may seem strange to you at first. After all, most moving objects that we observe stop after a while—they do not keep moving. However, the key to this law is the words *unless a force* (a push or a pull) *is applied.* There is a force on most moving objects. It is called friction, and it always pushes against the motion. If you stop pedaling your bicycle on a level path, you will continue to coast along for quite a distance, just as the first law of motion predicts. However, you will eventually stop. The friction between the bike's tires and the path reduces the velocity until it is finally zero.

The first law has a second part. The second part applies to objects that are not moving; objects that are at rest; objects with a velocity of zero. As you might guess, this part of the law states that objects at rest remain at rest unless a force is applied to them.

Newton's second law states that when a force is applied to an object, the object accelerates; that is, its velocity increases or decreases. (Some people refer to decreasing velocity as deceleration. Some call it negative acceleration. Whatever you call it, it is a change in velocity and, therefore, an acceleration.) The bigger the force acting on an object, the greater its acceleration. In fact, the acceleration is proportional to the force. If the force is doubled, the acceleration doubles. The acceleration also depends on the mass of the object to which a force is applied. Mass is the amount of matter in an object. A bowling ball has more mass than a baseball. If the same force is applied to different masses, objects with large masses will undergo smaller accelerations than those with small masses. A mass twice as big as another will have an acceleration half as large when both experience the same force. This law can be expressed mathematically as

$$\text{acceleration} = \text{force} \div \text{mass, or}$$

$$\text{acceleration} = \frac{\text{force}}{\text{mass}}, \text{ or } a = \frac{F}{m}.$$

If you put real numbers into this formula, you will see that doubling the force on the same mass doubles the acceleration. Otherwise, the equal sign is no longer valid. Similarly, if you double the mass, the acceleration halves.

Newton's third law of motion states that if one object exerts a force on a second object, the second object exerts an equal force on the first object, but in the opposite direction. This law might be called the "you push me, I'll push you" law. As you will see in Experiment 2-5, if I push you to the west, you will give me an equal push to the east, whether you want to or not.

2-1*
Basketball and Newton's First Law of Motion

Things you will need:

- basketball court or long hallway
- tennis ball
- basketball

Sometimes basketball players lose control of the ball as they dribble. They push it forward with too much or too little force. In this experiment, you will see how Newton's laws help you understand when the ball needs a forward force and when it does not.

Begin by walking along a basketball court or hallway with a tennis ball in your hand. (Start the experiment with a tennis ball because it is easier to catch in one hand than a basketball.) Let the ball fall from your hand as you walk. Without stopping, can you catch the ball as it rebounds? Does the ball keep moving forward with you after you drop it, or does it fall behind? How is the result of this experiment related to Newton's first law of motion?

Next, drop the tennis ball while standing still. At the moment you release the ball, begin to walk forward. Using Newton's first law, explain why the ball rebounds behind you.

Finally, as you walk, drop the ball again. But this time, stop walking immediately after you drop the ball. Using Newton's first law, explain why the ball moves ahead of you.

Now hold a basketball in your hands. As you start forward, drop the ball. As it rebounds, begin dribbling the ball as you walk forward. Do you have to push the ball forward to make it move with you, or can you simply push downward on the ball?

Continue to walk and dribble the basketball. Then, suddenly, after pushing the ball downward, begin to run. Do you think the ball will move with you or will it now be behind you?

What can you do to make the ball move with you if you suddenly begin to run? Remember, to start running you had to change your velocity—you had to accelerate.

While dribbling the ball as you run, suddenly stop. Again, to stop, you had to change your velocity—you had to accelerate. What happens to the ball when you stop? What do you have to do to keep the ball beside you?

From what you have found in this experiment, when should you apply a forward force on a basketball that you are dribbling? When should you apply a backward force on a basketball that you are dribbling?

Exploring on Your Own

Experiment 2-1 is very similar to one described by Galileo about four hundred years ago. He discovered that a ball dropped from the top of a moving ship's mast landed at the base of the mast; it did not fall behind the ship. He concluded that a moving object keeps its forward speed as it falls. You found the same thing to be true when you dropped a tennis ball or dribbled a basketball. As long as you walk at a steady speed, the ball will move with you. The ball will maintain its forward speed after you drop it.

If you have access to a large sailing vessel, you can repeat Galileo's experiment. If you do not, which is more likely, you can carry out a similar experiment inside one of the vehicles unknown to Galileo—a skateboard, bicycle, or in-line skates. Do your results agree with Galileo's?

Suppose you drop a ball while you make a turn. Where does the ball land? Can you explain what you observe? If not, try Experiments 2-6 and 2-7.

2-2*
More Sports and Newton's First Law of Motion

You can investigate Newton's first law of motion on a hockey rink. Stand at one end of the rink and use a hockey stick to shoot a puck along the length of the rink. Shoot the puck so that it stays on the ice as it moves. Try not to lift the puck as you shoot it. As you can see, the puck seems to move along at a constant speed, just as the first law states. But is it really moving at constant speed?

Things you will need:

- hockey rink
- hockey stick
- hockey puck
- 2 friends
- 2 stopwatches
- pen or pencil
- notebook

To find out, station one friend at center ice and a second friend at the opposite end of the rink from where you are standing. The distance between you and the friend at center ice should be the same as the distance between the friend at center ice and the friend at the other end of the rink. Each friend should have a stopwatch. At the moment you shoot the puck, both friends should start their stopwatches. The first friend should stop the watch at the moment the puck reaches center ice. The second friend should stop the watch at the moment the puck reaches him or her.

Record both readings on the stopwatches. Repeat the experiment several times and record all the data.

If the puck really travels at constant speed, how should the time for the puck to reach center ice compare with the time to reach the second friend at the other end of the rink? How do the times actually compare? What do the data tell you about the puck's velocity? Is the velocity constant? Does the puck's velocity decrease, increase, or stay the same as it moves? How do you know?

Exploring on Your Own

Do an experiment similar to Experiment 2-2 by rolling a basketball or a volleyball along an indoor court.

Do a similar experiment as you coast on a bicycle along a level pathway.

2-3*
Sports and the Second Part of Newton's First Law of Motion

As you remember, there was a second part to Newton's first law of motion. It applies to objects with a velocity of zero—objects that are at rest. You can test this law by placing a sheet of plastic on an old table or one that has a protective covering. Put a tennis racquet on the plastic, as shown in Figure 5. Allow part of the plastic to hang over the edge of the table.

Grasp the end of the plastic sheet in both hands, as shown. Then with a short, quick motion, pull the sheet toward you and downward.

Things you will need:

- sheet of plastic about 2 ft x 4 ft
- an old table or one that has a protective covering
- tennis racquet
- baseball glove

Figure 5. You can demonstrate the second part of Newton's first law of motion with a tennis racquet (or something similar that will not roll) resting on a sheet of plastic.

As you can see, the tennis racquet remains in place on the table. How does the second part of Newton's first law explain the result of this experiment? Is the result the same if you replace the tennis racquet with a baseball glove?

Exploring on Your Own

What happens if you pull the plastic sheet slowly instead of with a sudden jerk? How can you explain the difference? You may find some of the experiments in Chapter 4 provide useful information in answering this question.

2-4*
Sports and Newton's Second Law of Motion

As you know, Newton's second law may be expressed mathematically as

$$\text{acceleration} = \frac{\text{force}}{\text{mass}}, \text{ or } a = \frac{F}{m}.$$

To make an object accelerate (increase or decrease its speed), a force must be applied to it. In Experiment 2-1, you found that in dribbling a basketball, the ball would fall behind you when you started to run (accelerated). To keep the ball moving at your increasing pace, you had to apply a forward push (force) to the ball. Unless you apply a forward force to the ball, it will fall behind you, because it has no way of pushing itself.

If you think about it, a force had to act on you when you increased your velocity. This force came into play when you made yourself accelerate forward by pushing backward against the floor with your feet. As Newton's third law reveals, you received an equal force forward.

For a more direct look at Newton's second law, you can conduct an experiment on ice. The low friction of an icy surface will make the effects of small forces obvious on a skater who is pulled

Things you will need:

- icy surface or smooth level surface (if done on roller skates or in-line skates)
- 3 friends, two of whom can skate
- ice skates, roller skates, or in-line skates
- hockey or skating rink or frozen lake or pond, or roller-skating rink
- an adult if experiment is to be done on a frozen lake or pond
- long, heavy string or light rope
- spring balance (0-20 newton)—can probably be borrowed from school's science lab
- surface next to ice or smooth surface that has firm footing
- 3 sticks
- meterstick, yardstick, or tape measure
- stopwatch
- pen or pencil
- notebook

across the ice. The experiment can also be done with a person on roller skates or in-line skates, so long as he or she is on a level surface.

Have a friend on skates stand at one side of a hockey or skating rink or on a frozen lake or pond. **Check with an adult before you go onto a frozen lake or pond! It may not be safe.** Your friend should hold one end of a heavy string or light rope tightly against his or her body, several inches below the navel. In this way, when another friend pulls on the string, the force will act through your friend's center of gravity (see Chapter 3). By pulling through the center of gravity, the force will not tend to throw your friend off balance.

Attach a spring balance to the other end of the rope, as shown in Figure 6. The friend holding the spring balance should stand beyond the ice where he or she has firm footing and room to move away from the ice. Ask the friend with the spring balance to pull with a small but steady force. The force should be just strong enough to make the friend who is standing on skates begin to move with a *constant* velocity. Since there is no acceleration, the force that can be read on the spring balance is just equal to the force of friction. This force should be quite small, as it is applied to a person on skates. What is the frictional force between ice and skater?

Repeat the experiment with a force that is at least twice as large as the frictional force you discovered previously. Can you see that the skater accelerates?

Repeat the experiment once more with an even larger force. What effect does the larger force have on the skater's acceleration?

Keep the force the same but increase the mass. This can be done by having a second skater hold onto the belt of the skater who is being pulled. What effect does the larger mass have on the acceleration?

Measurements of acceleration are difficult to obtain with this experiment, but you can measure changes in average velocity during

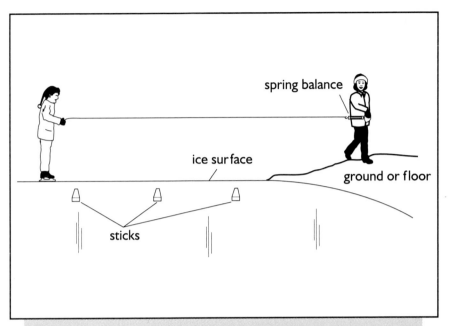

Figure 6. A person on skates is pulled with a constant force by another person who is on firm ground.

the time that a force acts on the skater. Place three sticks several meters apart on the level surface over which the skater will move. The distances between the sticks should be equal. One stick should be close to the point where the skater is standing, as shown in Figure 6. At the moment the skater moves past the first stick, start a stopwatch. Stop the watch when he or she reaches the second stick. Record that time. Have the skater return to his or her starting point and repeat the experiment while the same force is applied to the skater. This time, measure how long it takes for the skater to move from the second to the third stick, and record that time.

From the times and the distances, calculate the skater's average velocity between the first and the second stick. Then calculate his or her average velocity between the second and the third stick. Did the velocity increase as the skater moved under a constant force? Was the skater accelerating?

Exploring on Your Own

For an object that is being pulled by a constant force, develop a way to measure the velocity of that object at closely spaced intervals of time. Then use the data to plot a graph of velocity versus time. How can you find the object's acceleration from the graph?

Extend the experiment to show that Newton's second law holds true for a range of masses and forces.

2-5*
Sports and Newton's Third Law of Motion

As you know, Newton's third law is the "you push me, I'll push you" law. It states that if one object exerts a force on a second object, the second object exerts an equal force on the first object, but in the opposite direction. If you can skate, you can not only see but feel Newton's third law of motion.

Ask a friend who can also skate to join you on the ice, or on a smooth level surface if you are on roller skates or in-line skates.

Things you will need:

- friend who can skate

- skates

- ice or a smooth level surface if you are on roller skates or in-line skates

- an adult who can skate, who is much bigger than you

- something firmly fastened to the earth, such as the boards of a rink, a fence, a tree, or a building

Stand behind your friend while both of you are at rest. Place your hands against your friend's lower back, as shown in Figure 7. Tell your friend that you are going to give him or her a push forward. Then give that person a gentle push. As you might expect, your friend accelerates forward as you push. He or she then moves away at a steady speed once you are no longer in contact. But what happens to you? How do you know that your friend also exerted a force on you?

Repeat the experiment, but this time have your friend do the pushing. Are the results the same?

Repeat the experiment once more, but this time push harder. How are the results different? How are they the same?

Try the same experiment, pushing an adult who is much bigger than you. Considering the difference in mass, see if you can predict how the results will be different from your previous experiment. How are the results different? How are they the same?

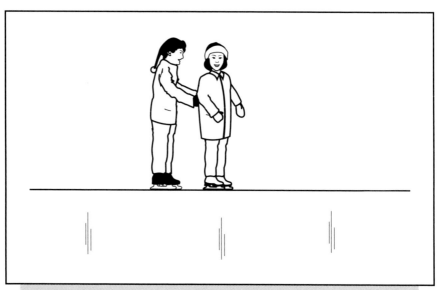

Figure 7. You can check Newton's third law of motion by pushing against a friend while both of you are at rest on skates.

Exploring on Your Own

Instead of pushing against another person on skates, push against something that is firmly fastened to the earth. You might push against the boards of the rink, a fence, a tree, or a building. Because these things are fastened to the earth, you are actually pushing against the whole earth. What happens when you conduct this experiment? How do you explain the results?

2-6
Sports and Forces Perpendicular to an Object's Motion

Things you will need:

• soccer ball

• open field

• a strong wind

• friend

• Ping-Pong ball

• table

• fan

You know that a force is needed to make something move. Do you know that a force is also needed to make a moving object change its direction?

If you gently kick a soccer ball that is at rest, you are not surprised to see the ball's speed increase when your foot makes contact with it. The ball accelerates as you would predict from Newton's second law. Neither would you be surprised to see the ball travel at nearly constant speed after it leaves your foot.

Of course, the ball will eventually come to rest, because friction between the ball and the air, and the ball and the ground is a force that pushes against the motion. To trap the ball, you apply a force that opposes the ball's motion, just as friction does to a lesser extent. The ball's speed decreases until it stops; in other words, the ball accelerates as you trap it. You may prefer to say the ball decelerates or has a negative acceleration. If you continue to apply force, the ball may even turn around and go the other way. As you can see, the direction that a force acts on a ball makes a difference in what happens to the ball.

When a strong wind is blowing, try kicking the ball: (a) against the wind; (b) with the wind; (c) across the wind (perpendicular to the wind's direction). How does the wind affect the motion of the ball in each case? Can wind exert a force on a ball? How do you know? If the wind is perpendicular to the ball's path, does it change the ball's speed? Does it change the ball's velocity?

To see more clearly how an object's motion is affected by a force perpendicular to its motion, try this. Have a friend gently kick

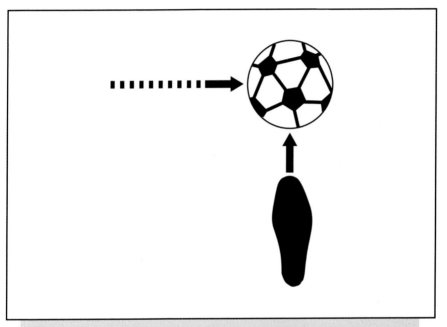

Figure 8. As the ball rolls by, apply a gentle kick perpendicular to the ball's motion. How does the force change the ball's path? Does the ball's speed change? Does its velocity change?

a soccer ball so that it rolls along the ground and past you. As it passes, give the ball a gentle kick sideways (perpendicular to its path), as shown in Figure 8. What path does the ball follow after you kick it? Did your force change the direction of the ball's path? Did the ball's speed change? Did its velocity change?

Try the same kind of experiment, using a Ping-Pong ball and table. Use a fan to blow air (a) against the ball's path; (b) in the direction the ball travels; (c) perpendicular to the ball's path. How does the moving air affect the motion of the ball in each case? Does the moving air push on a ball? How do you know? If the fan blows air perpendicular to the ball's path, does it change the ball's speed? Does it change the ball's velocity? Does the ball accelerate?

2-7
Making Circles on Ice

When a force acts on a ball or any other object, the object accelerates in the direction of the force. If the object is at rest, it begins to move. Should the object be moving, its velocity increases if the force is in the direction it is moving. If the force opposes the motion, as happens with friction, its speed decreases. When the force is perpendicular to the direction of the object's motion, the speed does not change, but the direction of the motion does. An object moving in a circle at constant speed is always changing its direction because of a force that pulls it inward. We call this inward force a *centripetal* force (from the Latin *centripetus*, meaning center-seeking).

Things you will need:

- clear plastic vial and cover
- water
- turntable
- clear plastic tape
- bicycle
- bicycle helmet
- large, smooth, level area, such as an unoccupied parking lot
- friend who skates
- ice rink or frozen pond
- an adult if using frozen pond
- skates

The inward acceleration on an object moving in a circle can be detected with an accelerometer. An accelerometer also shows you the direction of the force, because the force is always in the same direction as the acceleration.

You can make an accelerometer quite easily. All you need is a clear plastic vial and cover, as shown in Figure 9a. Fill the vial with water so that only a small bubble of air is left inside. Put the cap back on the vial. Turn the vial so that it is horizontal instead of vertical. Then push the vial forward lengthwise along a level surface. You will see the bubble move forward in the direction of the acceleration and force. When the vial stops (decelerates), you will see the bubble move backward, again in the direction of the acceleration and force.

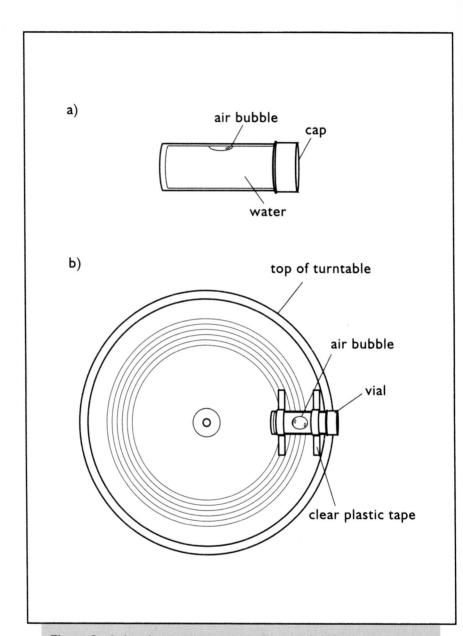

Figure 9. a) A vial containing water and an air bubble can serve as an accelerometer. b) Mount the accelerometer on a turntable. Which way does the bubble move when the turntable is rotating? What is the direction of the force and acceleration of an object when it moves in a circle?

Now hold the vial level so the bubble is in the center of the vial, as shown in Figure 9a, or tip it slightly so that the bubble is at the far end of the vial. Then turn around in a circle and watch the bubble as you turn. How does it move? What is the direction of the acceleration when the vial moves in a circle?

Tape the vial to a turntable with clear plastic tape, as shown in Figure 9b. Which way does the bubble move when the turntable spins? What is the direction of the acceleration and force on an object when it moves in a circle?

To make anything move along a curved path or arc, there must be a force directed toward the center of that circular path. In this experiment, you will see how a hockey player obtains the centripetal force needed to turn on ice. But first, look at this force while biking— a sport that most athletes engage in, if only informally.

Find a large, smooth, level area such as an *unoccupied* parking lot. There you can ride and experiment without danger. **Remember to wear your helmet.** Ride at moderate speed along a straight path. To make the bicycle move along a circular path, you lean inward. This causes part of your weight to push outward against the ground along which the bicycle tires are moving. Newton's third law tells us that the ground will push inward with a force equal to the outward force that the tires exert against the ground. This inward force is the centripetal force that keeps the bicycle and rider moving along a curved path.

Watch a friend on skates as he or she moves along a curved path on ice. Does the skater lean inward? Does the skater's lead skate push outward against the ice? What is the direction of the force that the ice exerts on the skate? What may happen if the skates are not sharp?

A player asked his hockey coach how to turn quickly on ice. The coach replied, "Lower your inside shoulder—the shoulder on the side toward which you want to turn. At the same time, push outward on the skate in front of you, which should be on your inside foot. Bring your outside skate around your leaning body so that it becomes the lead skate and push outward on it."

Try following the coach's instruction while you are skating. Does it work? What provides the force that allows you to travel along curved paths while moving fast on skates?

How can you make a hockey puck follow a circular path?

2-8*
Curveballs

Anybody can throw a curveball. All you have to do is throw a ball. Gravity will make it curve downward along a path like the one you see in Figure 10a. But baseball pitchers can throw balls that curve to the right or left as they travel from the pitcher's mound to home plate (Figure 10bi). Sometimes they throw a ball that falls faster or slower than it normally would (see Figures 10bii and iii). If you are a pitcher, perhaps you can throw a curveball or a sinker. But whether

or not you can throw curves, you know about Newton's laws of motion. Since you are aware of these laws, you know that there must be a force other than gravity acting on the ball if it curves left or right or falls faster or slower than it normally would. It was Newton himself, a tennis player, who first explained how a moving ball can be made to curve.

To see what makes a ball curve, hold a large Styrofoam ball or a beach ball in both hands. As you push the ball forward with your arms, give it some spin by pushing forward with one hand and pulling backward with the other. This will make the ball spin clockwise or counterclockwise after it leaves your hand. Throw the ball this way several times.

Watch the ball closely after you throw it. Does the ball curve? Which way does it curve? Throw the ball again, but this time make it spin in the opposite direction. Which way does it curve this time?

Next, try to throw a curveball, using a Styrofoam ball about the size of a baseball. Turn your wrist as you throw the ball so that it is

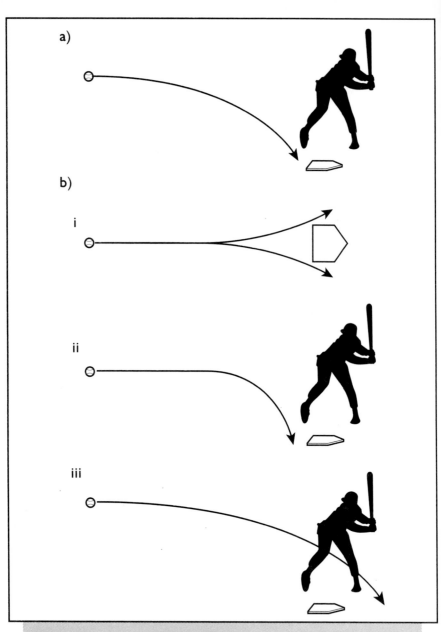

Figure 10. a) Side view of a thrown ball that is pulled downward by the force of gravity as it reaches home plate. b) (i) Top view of a ball that curves to the right or left of its normal straight-line path. (ii) Side view of "drop"—a ball that curves downward faster than it would due to gravity alone. (iii) Side view of a "rising" fastball—a ball that curves downward more slowly than it would as a result of gravity.

spinning after you release it. Does the ball curve? Now try it with a baseball or a softball. Can you make that ball curve?

Sometimes it is useful to kick a soccer ball so that it takes a curved path around an opponent. You can kick a curve by making the inside of your foot strike the ball to the left or right of the ball's center. Bring your foot across the ball as you make contact so that the ball spins to the left or right. What path does the kicked ball follow when you do this? How can you make it curve the other way?

If you play tennis or table tennis, how can you put spin on a ball that you are serving an opponent? How can you hit the ball with your racquet or paddle so that it curves to the left? How can you make it curve to the right?

As Newton explained, a spinning ball causes the air pressure on one side of the ball to become greater than the air pressure on the other side. This difference in pressure makes the ball curve right or left. If the ball has a counterclockwise spin (as viewed from above) when it moves away from you, air builds up on the right side of the ball. Because the right side of the ball is moving in the same direction as the ball, air molecules are caught up on the ball's surface. This increases the concentration of air molecules on the right side of the ball. The increased pressure on the ball's right side pushes it to the left. How should the ball be thrown to make it curve to the right?

Exploring on Your Own

Design an experiment to find out how the distance that a baseball is deflected left or right is affected by the rate at which the ball is spinning.

Design an experiment to find out how the distance that a spinning baseball is deflected left or right is affected by the speed at which the ball is moving.

3

Sports, Balance, Centers of Gravity, and Friction

The center of gravity (COG) of any object is the point where all its weight can be considered to be located. It is the point from which the object, if suspended, will be balanced with no tendency to rotate. Every object has a COG, but it is not necessarily at the center of the object. To see what this means and how COG is related to sports, you can begin by doing Experiment 3-1.

3-1
An Object's Center of Gravity

Place a ruler on your index finger. Where must your finger be for the ruler to balance? Where do you think the ruler's COG is located? Why do you think it is more difficult to balance the ruler if you place its *end* on your fingertip?

From a sheet of cardboard, cut an irregularly shaped object similar to the one in Figure 11. To find the object's COG, pin it to a bulletin board so that it is free to turn. Place the pin near the edge of the irregular shape, as shown in the drawing. You can make a plumb line by tying a metal washer or lead sinker to a long length of thread. Tie the plumb line to the pin, as shown in the drawing. A plumb line will always hang so that it is directed toward the center of the earth. Use a pencil or pen to draw a line behind the thread on the cardboard. Then rotate the cardboard and put the pin near the top edge again. Make another line along the cardboard behind the thread. Repeat this several times.

Notice that the lines you have drawn all cross at a single point. You might guess that this point is the object's COG. To see if you are right, mark the point and remove the pin. Now try to balance the cardboard sheet by placing your finger beneath that point. Will the cardboard, when horizontal, balance with your fingertip beneath it at that point? Will it balance at any other point? Where is the COG of the cardboard sheet?

Stack three cubic blocks and tape them together, as shown in Figure 12a. Where is the COG of the three blocks? Keep your eye

Things you will need:

- flat ruler
- sheet of cardboard
- shears
- straight pin
- bulletin board
- metal washer or lead sinker
- thread
- pencil or pen
- 3 cubic blocks
- tape
- protractor

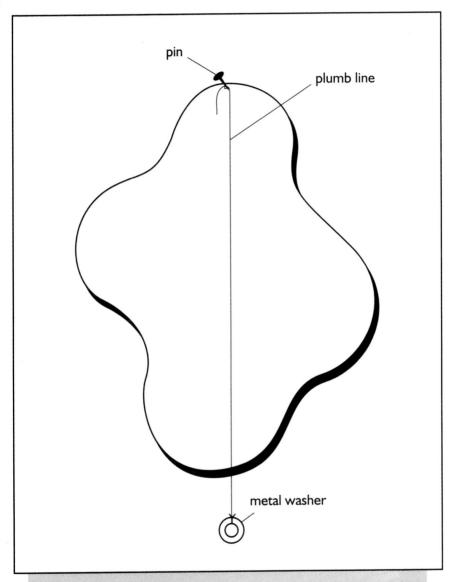

Figure 11. A plumb line attached to the top of an irregularly shaped object is free to turn. The line will always cross the object's center of gravity.

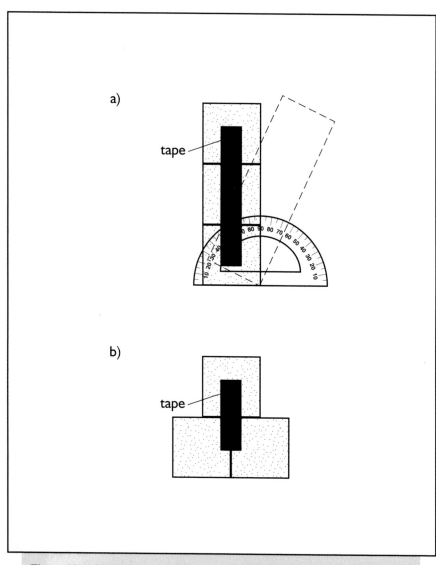

Figure 12. a) Through what angle must you tip these blocks before they fall over? Where is the COG of the three blocks when they begin to topple? b) How does lowering an object's COG and widening its base affect the angle required to tip the blocks over?

on the COG as you tip the blocks. Use a protractor to measure the angle through which they have to be tipped before they fall over. Remove one of the blocks so the object is only two blocks high. Where is the COG of the two blocks? Watch the COG again as you tip the blocks. Through what angle must the two blocks be tipped before they fall over?

Next, tape the blocks so the base is two blocks wide and the third block is centered above the other two (Figure 12b). Where is the COG now? Through what angle must these blocks be tipped before they topple?

From what you have seen in this experiment, what happens to an object when its COG does not lie over the base of the object? How does lowering an object's COG affect its stability—the angle it must be tipped to make it fall? How does widening an object's base affect its stability?

3-2
Your Center of Gravity

Where do you think your center of gravity is located? To find out, place a thick pillow on the top of the back of a chair or find a chair with a soft, padded back. **Ask an adult** to hold the chair while you balance your body

horizontally on the back of the chair, as shown in Figure 13. Where on your body do you think your balance point is located? Where do you think your COG is located? Most people's COG is several inches below their navel and halfway through their body.

Now that you know the approximate position of your COG, see what happens when your COG does not lie above your base (foot

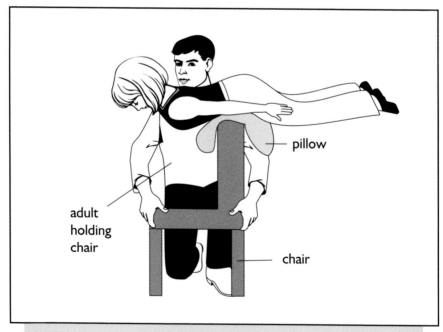

Figure 13. Ask an adult to hold a chair while you find your body's balance point.

or feet). Stand on soft carpeting with your left side beside a vertical wall. Your left foot and shoulder should touch the wall. What happens when you try to lift your right leg? Can you explain why it happens?

Now stand with your back and both heels against the wall. What happens when you try to bend down to touch your toes? Can you explain why it happens?

Stand in front of a full-length mirror. Watch what happens to your body when you lift one foot off the floor. Turn sideways. Then watch what happens to your body when you bend down and touch your toes. How does your body adjust to keep your COG over its base?

3-3*
Sports and Center of Gravity

Football players are coached to take a wide stance (feet apart) and keep the center of their bodies low when they get into position. When tackling an

Things you will need:
- grassy area where ground is soft and flat
- friend

opponent, they are often instructed to keep their eyes on a point several inches below the center of the ball carrier's waist. Players who carry the ball are told to run with a wide base and to stay low.

Soccer players are coached to take a wide stance while heading a ball, to keep the center of their bodies low when approaching an offensive player with the ball, and to watch a point several inches below the center of that offensive player's waist.

Hockey players are told to keep their skates as far apart as the width of their shoulders, to keep the center of their bodies low when approaching an offensive player with the puck, and to watch a point several inches below that offensive player's waist.

Is there a good reason for such coaching tips? Why are players coached to run and position themselves in this way?

To see what such coaching tips have to do with your COG, stand on a soft, grassy area with your feet together. Ask a friend to give you a shoulder-level push to one side. What happens?

Repeat the experiment, but this time stand with your feet spread well apart. Why are you more stable in this position?

Repeat the experiment once more, but this time stand with your feet spread well apart and your knees bent so that your body is much lower. Why are you even more stable in this position?

Exploring on Your Own

Why do coaches tell players to watch an opponent's COG (a point several inches below the center of their waists) rather than some other part of their body, to avoid being deceived?

Gymnasts have a particular concern for COG. What happens when a gymnast's COG is not over the balance beam?

How can you determine where the COG of a baseball is located?

How can you determine where the COG of a football is located?

3-4*
A Football's Center of Gravity and Passing

When someone says "ball," you probably think of a sphere—something round like a globe. Most of the balls used in sports are round. The game of football

is different. It is played with a ball that looks like two fat miniature canoes that have been glued together. Throwing or kicking a football is a whole different ball game. To make a football travel far and true requires skill.

The COG of a spherical ball is at its center, but a football is not a sphere. Its COG is inside the ball at the center of the circle around the ball's fattest part. If you punt a football by bringing your foot against the ball's COG, the ball will "float"; it will not rotate. Try punting a ball this way. You will see that it floats and does not travel very far.

Throwing a football requires skill. Try throwing it with your hand behind the ball's center of gravity (COG). The COG of any object is the point where all its weight can be considered to be located. To throw a football so that your hand pushes through the ball's COG, place your hand perpendicular to the ball's longest axis, at its fattest part. When you throw the ball this way, you will be pushing along the ball's COG. Throw the ball to a friend. Notice that the ball floats like a knuckleball in baseball.

How far can you throw a football when you throw it with your hand directly behind its COG? How accurately can you throw the football?

Now throw the ball as a quarterback would. Grasp the ball by its laces at points behind its COG, as shown in Figure 14a. If you throw the ball that way, you can make it spiral; that is, you can make the ball spin about the long axis through its COG, as shown in Figure 14b.

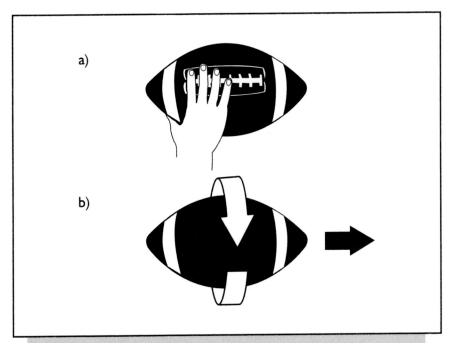

Figure 14. a) To throw a spiral, hold the ball by its laces at points behind its COG. b) With this grip you can throw a spiral; that is, you can make the ball rotate about its COG.

How far can you throw a football when you throw a spiral? How accurately can you throw the football when you make it spiral? Can you throw farther and more accurately when you make it spiral than when you throw a "floater"?

If possible, repeat the experiment with different people throwing the football. Are the results the same?

Exploring on Your Own

If a force is applied at any object's COG, a football or anything else, the object will not rotate. To throw a spiral as a quarterback does, a force must be applied at some distance from the COG. Such a force causes the ball to rotate about its COG. The same thing happens when you pull on the rim of a wheel that is free to spin.

Any object rotating about its COG is said to have angular momentum. Carry out an investigation to find out what momentum and angular momentum have to do with the constant rotation of a thrown football. What role does gravity play when a football is thrown?

How does the pointed shape of a football affect its flight through the air from passer to receiver?

3-5*
A Football's Center of Gravity and Kicking

Things you will need:

- football
- large field or lawn
- kicking tee
- a friend

As you know from Experiment 3-4, the COG of a football is inside the ball at the center of the circle around the ball's fattest part. If you punt a football by bringing your foot's instep through the ball's COG, what do you predict will happen to the ball? Try punting the ball this way. Does it move the way you predicted it would?

Now try punting the ball by bringing your foot *across* the ball as you kick through its COG. Why should this make the ball spiral? How does the distance and accuracy of spiral punts compare with that of floaters?

Place the ball upright on a kicking tee. What do you predict will happen if you kick the ball that is resting on the tee through its COG? Try it! Was your prediction correct?

How do you predict the ball will travel if you kick it below its COG? Above its COG? Try kicking it both ways. Were your predictions correct?

Exploring on Your Own

Onside kicks are often made late in a game during a kickoff by a team that is behind. The kicking team tries to recover the free ball after it has gone 10 yards. The third bounce of such a kick is often very high, giving the kicking team time to run under it and recover it.

Investigate this third bounce. How can it be higher than previous bounces? What must happen to the ball's kinetic (motion) energy when it bounces higher than before? Can such a bounce be explained by scientific principles?

3-6*
A Baseball or Softball Bat, Its COG, and Its Sweet Spot

Baseball and softball players talk about the "sweet spot" on a bat. The sweet spot is the place on the bat where the batter likes to make contact with the ball. It

Things you will need:
- wooden baseball or softball bat
- hammer
- marking pens

feels good when you make contact with the ball on the sweet spot. If the bat collides with the ball at other points, the bat vibrates. In cold weather, the vibrations may cause the batter's hands to sting. If the bat vibrates, some of the kinetic energy (the energy associated with motion) you use to hit the ball goes into the vibrating bat rather than into the ball. When you hit the ball at the sweet spot, the maximum amount of kinetic energy is transferred to the ball, so it will go farther.

Is the sweet spot at the same place as the bat's COG? You might guess that it is. In this experiment you can find the sweet spot and see for yourself if the COG and sweet spot are one and the same.

To begin, find the COG of a baseball or softball bat by balancing the bat on your index finger, as shown in Figure 15a. Use a marking pen to mark the bat's COG.

Next, find the bat's sweet spot, the spot where there are no vibrations when the bat and a ball collide. Hold the bat with your fingers loosely surrounding its narrow end. The bat should be free to swing, as shown in Figure 15b. With a hammer, tap the bat gently at a point close to its fat end. You will feel the bat's vibration in your fingertips. Continue tapping the bat at different places with the hammer. When you tap the sweet spot, you will feel no vibration.

Mark the location of the sweet spot on the bat with a marking pen. Is the bat's sweet spot located at the same place as its COG?

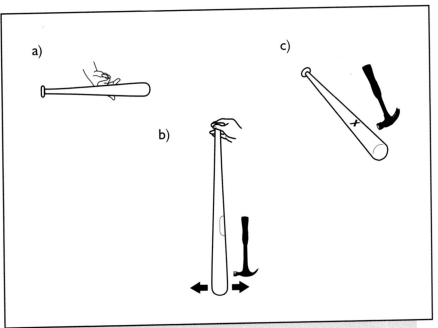

a)

c)

b)

X

Figure 15. a) Find a bat's COG by balancing it on your finger. b) You can find the sweet spot on a bat by tapping it gently with a hammer. c) How does the bat move when you hit it at its COG? How does the bat move when you hit it at its sweet spot?

Exploring on Your Own

Place the bat on the floor. Use a hammer to tap the horizontal bat at its COG. (See Figure 15c.) How does the bat move when you strike it on its COG? How does it move when you strike it at the sweet spot?

Can you explain why the bat moves as it does when you hit its COG? Can you explain why the bat moves as it does when you hit its sweet spot?

3-7
Why Do Baseball and Softball Players Slide?

In baseball and softball, sliding is a major part of the game. Players usually slide when they steal a base or try to take an extra base on a batted ball. But why does a player slide? Does sliding increase the player's speed?

Things you will need:

- toy truck about six inches long with rubber wheels
- wide rubber bands
- smooth, level surface

To find out, give a toy truck a push and watch it roll along a smooth, level floor. The rolling truck corresponds to a base runner running from first base in an attempt to steal second.

Next, wrap a wide rubber band around the front and rear tires of the truck. This will prevent the wheels from turning. Push the truck again with the same force you used before. Since the wheels cannot turn, the truck will slide, not roll, along the floor. The sliding truck represents the player sliding into second base. Did the sliding truck move faster or slower than it did when its wheels were free to roll along the floor?

Perhaps you can better answer the question of why base runners slide after you think about another question: What would happen to a player trying to steal second if he or she did not slide? Finally, why, in general, do players not slide into first base?

3-8
Friction and Football Cleats

Friction is the force between two surfaces, such as the force between your shoes and the floor. Frictional forces always oppose motion. Often, it is the force of friction that brings a moving body to rest. On the other hand, it is friction that enables us to move. Normally, when you walk, you push back against the earth with your foot. The earth, as expected from Newton's third law of motion, pushes forward on your foot, and you move. If you were to find yourself on a truly frictionless frozen pond, you would be unable to walk. Without friction, there would be no way that you could push against the ice.

As you found in Experiment 2-5, our ability to walk or run on the earth can be found in Newton's third law of motion. When one object pushes another, the second object exerts an *equal* but oppositely directed force on the first. If I push you, you automatically push me in the opposite direction. Since the forces are the same, each body acquires the same momentum. (Momentum is a property of a moving body. It is equal to the body's mass times its velocity.) If one body is heavy and the other light, the lighter body will move away with more speed than the heavier one.

Football players must be able to push hard against the earth in order to push hard against an opponent during a block or tackle. Cleats enable them to get a firm grip on the earth. Because the earth is so much more massive than even the world's heaviest football player, the velocity of the earth when a player pushes against it is negligible compared with the speed the player attains. But what would happen if the player could not push against the earth? You will find out in this experiment.

Stand on a floor, sidewalk, or lawn and walk along that surface. Notice that as you walk, your rear foot on each step pushes back against the surface as the other foot is lifted and swung forward. Since the surface is attached to the earth, you are really pushing back against the earth as you walk.

To find out what would happen if you could not push against the earth, place a long, wide board on some wooden dowels. The board and dowels should be on a smooth, level surface. Place some of the dowels behind the board, as shown in Figure 16. **Have an adult** stand beside you as you do this experiment (the adult is there to catch you if you should start to fall). What happens when you try to walk on such a small "earth"?

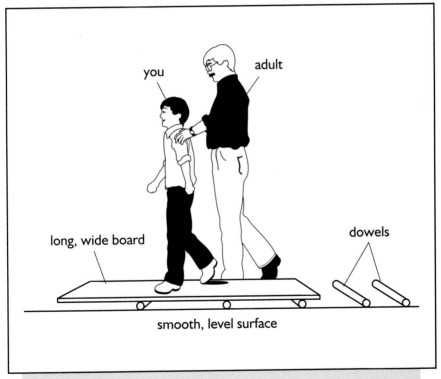

Figure 16. What happens when you try to walk on a very light "earth"?

3-9*
Friction and "English"

In Experiment 2-8, you learned how pitchers throw curveballs. The secret is in the way the ball is made to spin as it moves through air. But baseballs often take funny hops after being hit. These abnormal bounces are also caused by the ball's spinning. But

Things you will need:

- Styrofoam ball about three inches in diameter
- smooth concrete floor
- basketball
- basketball court

here it is the friction between the spinning ball and the surface it hits that produces the different bounce. With experience, a fielder learns what kind of spin to expect on various batted balls. Knowing the spin, the fielder can predict how the ball will bounce when it hits the ground. Tennis players sometimes put "English" on the ball when they hit it with their racquets. The spin causes the ball to take abnormal bounces. In any sport where the ball can be made to spin, bounces can be tricky.

To see how a ball normally bounces, throw a Styrofoam ball onto a smooth concrete floor with as little spin as possible. You will see that the ball bounces up from the floor at about the same angle it hit the floor (Figure 17a).

Next, launch the ball with lots of topspin. This is best done by using two hands, one under and one on top of the ball. As the ball is launched, use your top hand to apply a forward (top) spin, as shown in Figure 17b. How does the bounce of the ball with topspin compare with the bounce it took when there was no spin?

Next, throw the ball with backspin. As the ball is launched, use your top hand to apply a backward (back) spin, as shown in Figure 17c. How does this ball's bounce compare with the others?

Exploring on Your Own

From what you have discovered about topspin and backspin, see if you can make the ball bounce to the right of its original direction.

78

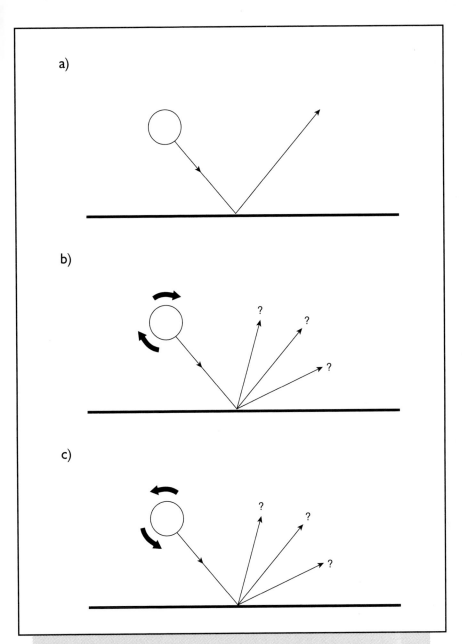

Figure 17. a) The path of a bouncing ball that is not spinning. b) What path will a ball with topspin follow after it bounces? c) What path will a ball with backspin follow after it bounces?

Can you make it bounce to the left of its original direction? Can you make the ball bounce backward?

Using Newton's first and third laws of motion and the frictional force between ball and floor, explain the bounce you observed when the ball had very little spin. Explain the bounce the ball took when it had topspin. Explain the bounce the ball took when it had backspin. What forces and laws of motion explain your ability to make the ball bounce left, right, or even backward?

Carry out some experiments to see how the spin you apply to a Ping-Pong ball can be used to control the ball's motion and make it follow nonlinear paths.

Many basketball players recommend putting backspin on the ball when a shot is made. Try taking some shots at the basket with a basketball. Stand at a distance where your shooting percentage is good. Try putting topspin, backspin, sidespin, and no spin on your shots. Does it work as you would predict from what you know about spinning balls, friction, and Newton's laws of motion? What advantage does a player have if he or she applies backspin to the ball when making a shot from the field or foul line?

4

Sports, Momentum, and Collisions

The momentum of a ball or of any moving object is its mass times its velocity (mass x velocity, or *mv*).

Momentum = mass x velocity, or $M = mv$

If you have a mass of 50 kilograms (kg) and are running at a velocity of 6 meters per second (m/s), your momentum is 300 kg·m/s.

The momentum of a ball (or any object) depends on the impulse it receives. Impulse is the product of the force applied to the ball and the time that the force acts.

Impulse = force x time, or $I = Ft$

If a net force of 100 newtons (N) acts on you for 3 seconds, you receive an impulse of 300 N·s.

Since an object receives its momentum from the impulse applied to it, the two quantities are equal; that is:

Momentum = Impulse, or $mv = Ft$.

The greater the impulse applied to an object, such as a ball, the greater its momentum. You know that when a force acts on an object at rest, the object accelerates in the direction of the force. As the velocity of the object increases, so does its momentum. As long as the force acts, the object continues to accelerate. Consequently, the longer a certain force acts on a ball, the more momentum the ball acquires.

Suppose a force, F, is applied to a ball for a time, t. The ball acquires a certain momentum, mv, that is equal to Ft. You can give the ball the same momentum by applying a force twice as big for half as much time. Or you can give the ball the same momentum by applying a force half as big for twice as long.

If you tried to stop a car rolling slowly along a level surface, you could not stop the car quickly because you are not strong enough to apply a force big enough to stop the car in a short time. However, if you tied a rope to the car and pulled back against its motion, you could eventually bring it to rest.

4-1*
Sports, Follow-Through, and Momentum

Coaches often tell players to "follow through!" But what does *follow through* mean, and how important is it? From what you know about impulse and momentum, you may be able to figure out the scientific meaning of follow-through by doing some experiments related to different sports. You can begin with soccer.

Things you will need:

- soccer ball
- large field or lawn
- hockey rink or smooth, frozen lake or pond
- hockey stick
- hockey puck
- an adult if using outdoor ice
- football

Follow-Through and Soccer

One way to discover the effect of following through is to kick a soccer ball. Kick the ball with your instep as you normally would during a warm-up period. That is, kick the ball with a fluid, but not swift, leg motion and continue to move your foot and leg forward and upward after it makes contact with the ball.

Next, kick the ball without following through. Stop your foot's motion at the moment it makes contact with the ball.

Make a few more kicks, some with good follow-through, others without follow-through. Does following through increase the distance the ball travels?

If you are a soccer goalie, how can you do the same experiment by throwing the ball with and without follow-through?

Follow-Through and Hockey

Hockey coaches tell players to "follow through" when they shoot the puck. They mean keep the stick on the puck for as long as possible. Do not stop driving the puck midway through the process of shooting. As you shoot, shift your weight from your rear foot to your front foot. This will increase the speed of your shot.

To see the effect of following through while shooting a hockey puck, begin by shooting the puck as you normally would in making a slap shot. That is, draw your stick back to the height of your hips, swing it into the puck, and turn your wrists so as to keep the stick against the puck for as long as possible. As you move the stick and your arms forward after striking the puck, shift your weight from your rear foot to your front foot just as you would if you were throwing a ball.

Next, shoot the puck without any follow-through. Stop the motion of the stick and your arms and the forward transfer of your weight at the moment the stick makes contact with the puck.

Make a few more shots, some with good follow-through, others without follow-through. How does following through affect the speed of the puck?

Follow-Through and Football

Another way to see the effect of following through is to punt a football or kick it from a kicking tee. After you have stretched and warmed up, punt a football or kick it from a tee as you normally would in a game. That is, kick the ball with a fluid forward leg motion that continues after your foot makes contact with the ball.

Next, kick the ball without following through. That is, stop your foot's motion at the moment it makes contact with the ball. Do not continue to move your foot through the ball after the initial contact.

Make a few more kicks, some with good follow-through, others without follow-through. Does following through increase the distance the ball travels? How is follow-through related to the impulse you apply to the ball?

Exploring on Your Own

Examine follow-through as it applies to tennis, table tennis, basketball, baseball or softball, lacrosse, golf, and other sports of your choice.

Return to Experiment 2-3. Using your knowledge of impulse, explain why the results of that experiment were so dependent on the size of the force you applied to the plastic.

In addition to impulse, what other factors are involved in Experiment 2-3?

Now that you are familiar with forces, momentum, and impulses, think again about Experiment 1-8, where you measured running speed on soft and hard surfaces. Explain why athletes run more slowly on soft fields than on hard fields. How is the time for a runner's foot to come to rest with each step related to the firmness of the field's surface? How is the upward force on the athlete's foot affected by the softness or hardness of the field's turf?

4-2
Sports, Impulse, and Catching

Catching or trapping a ball is part of many sports. Coaches often say that players who catch or trap well have "soft hands" or "soft feet." What do coaches mean by "soft"?

Find out what it is like to be on the receiving end of a pass in a number of different sports. You might begin with baseball, where catching is the fundamental defensive part of the game.

Things you will need:

- baseball glove
- friend
- baseball
- soccer ball
- hockey sticks
- hockey pucks
- hockey rink or frozen lake or pond
- an adult if using outdoor ice

Catching and Baseball

Put on a baseball glove. Ask a friend to throw you a baseball with moderate speed. (**DO NOT try this experiment with a fastball!**) Keep your hand and glove in a fixed position as you catch the ball.

Repeat the experiment, but this time let your hand, arm, and glove move with the ball as you catch it (see Figure 18). This is the way someone catches a baseball if he or she has no glove—the way a smart fan in the bleachers catches a foul ball. It is the way a first baseman catches a hard throw or the way any fielder catches a line drive.

Repeat the experiment a few times. Which method of catching the ball—stiff- or loose-handed—requires you to apply a bigger force to the ball? How can you tell? In which case did it take longer to make the catch? How do you know?

In both ways of catching the ball, you transferred the ball's momentum—its mass times its velocity—to your body and ultimately to the earth on which you stood. In both cases you applied a force to the ball. In both ways of catching the ball, the force acted

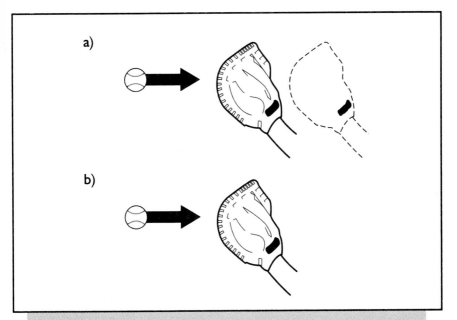

Figure 18. a) To increase the time that you apply a force to a ball as you catch it, let your hand and glove move with the ball. b) A rigidly held glove will reduce the time you apply a force to the ball in catching it.

on the ball for a short interval. In both ways of catching the ball, you applied an impulse—a force times a time—to the ball. When you caught the ball by moving your arm, hand, and glove with the ball, you increased the time that the force acted on the ball. Which method of catching the ball took the sting out of the catch? Why? Which method of catching the ball reduced your chances of dropping it? Why?

Catching, Trapping, and Soccer

Like baseball and football players who are adept at catching balls, a good soccer goalie must have soft hands, too. Of course, soccer players who are not goalies are not allowed to use their hands except on throw-ins, but they do have to trap balls with their bodies, legs, and head. It would not be right to say they have soft bodies, and certainly not soft heads, but they do have to let their bodies, legs, or heads move with the ball as they trap it.

To see why they do, ask a friend to throw or kick a soccer ball to you. The ball should travel at a moderate speed. Keep your body or leg in a fixed position as you trap the ball. **DO NOT try to trap the ball with your head in this way!**

Repeat the experiment, but this time let your body or leg move with the ball as you trap it.

Repeat the experiment a few times. Which method of trapping the ball required you to apply a bigger force to the ball? How could you tell? Why should you let your body, legs, or head move with the ball when you trap it?

In both ways of trapping the ball, you transferred the ball's momentum—its mass times its velocity—to your body and ultimately to the earth on which you stood. In both cases you applied a force to the ball. In both ways of trapping the ball, the force acted on the ball for a short interval. In both ways of trapping, you applied an impulse—a force over time—to the ball. When you trapped the ball by moving your leg or body with the ball, you increased the time that the force acted on the ball. Which method of trapping the ball felt better? Why? Which method of catching the ball reduced your chances of losing it to an opponent? Why?

Receiving a Pass in Hockey

A hockey goalie catching a puck is similar to a catcher receiving a fastball, but the other members of a hockey team receive the puck in a very different way. Stand on a hockey rink or any smooth, icy surface, with a hockey stick in your hands. Ask a friend to use his or her stick to pass a puck swiftly along the ice to you. As the puck reaches your stick, use your arms to keep the stick in a firmly fixed position on the ice. What happens to the puck when it hits your stick?

Repeat the experiment, but this time let the stick move with the puck as you receive it. What happens to the puck this time?

Repeat each method of receiving the puck a few times. In which method of receiving the puck—with a fixed stick or a loose-handed stick—do you apply a bigger force to the puck? How can you tell? Which method of receiving the puck takes longer? Which is the better way to receive a puck? Why?

In both ways of receiving the puck you transferred the puck's momentum—its mass times its velocity—to your body through the stick and ultimately to the earth through your body. In both cases you applied a force to the moving puck. In both ways of receiving it, the force acted on the puck for a period of time. In both ways of receiving the puck, you applied an impulse—a force over time—to it. When you received the puck by letting the stick "give" with the puck, you increased the time that the force acted on the puck. In which method of receiving the puck did you feel less force on your hands through the stick? Why? Which method of receiving the puck reduced your chances of losing it to an opponent? Why?

Collisions in Sports

Collisions are common in sports. Collisions between players are part of the game in football and hockey. Collisions between balls and bats occur in baseball and softball. Collisions between balls and racquets constitute the games of tennis, squash, and racquetball. Collisions between a ball and a surface are part of any game played with a ball.

For a collision to occur, one or more of the objects that collide must be in motion. During collisions, impulses are applied to bring about changes in momentum. There are also energy transformations during a collision. Part of the energy of motion (kinetic energy) may be changed to elastic energy within the materials that bump into one another. For example, when a ball collides with a floor, materials within the ball are squeezed together (compressed) during the collision. This is similar to a spring being compressed. Energy is stored in the spring. It reappears as the spring returns to its normal length.

As the elastic material in a ball returns to its normal shape during the rebound, some of the elastic energy is changed back to kinetic energy. The rest appears as thermal energy (the ball becomes warmer).

If all the kinetic energy is restored after a collision, the collision is said to be elastic. Collisions among gas molecules or between gas molecules and the walls of their containers are completely elastic. We do not have to add energy to keep them from slowing down. If *all* the kinetic energy is lost during a collision, such as the collision between a lump of clay and the floor, the collision is said to be totally inelastic. Many collisions are partially elastic, meaning some kinetic energy is regained after the collision.

4-3*
Collisions Between Surfaces and Balls Used in Sports

Things you will need:
- Superball
- rubber ball
- Styrofoam ball
- clay
- yardstick or meterstick
- hard floor or sidewalk
- notebook
- pen or pencil
- balls used in a variety of sports, such as baseball, softball, Ping-Pong, basketball, golf, handball, lacrosse, soccer, squash, tennis, etc.
- friend

Playing the bounce is a part of any sport in which a ball is used. But the balls used in some sports are bouncier than those used in others. In this experiment, you will test the bounciness (elasticity) of different balls. Try to determine which of the collisions you observe are more or less elastic than others.

Have a friend hold a yardstick or meterstick upright on a hard floor or sidewalk, as shown in Figure 19. Hold a Superball so that the bottom of the ball is level with the top of the yardstick or meterstick. Then release the ball. Have your friend watch the ball closely as it rebounds. To what height does the bottom of the ball rise after it collides with the floor?

Repeat the experiment several times to make sure the results are nearly the same each time. How high does the ball bounce? Record the result in your notebook.

To what fraction of its original height does the ball rise? Is the collision completely elastic? Is it completely inelastic? How high would it bounce if the collision were completely elastic?

Repeat the experiment, using a rubber ball, a Styrofoam ball, and a ball made from clay. How does the elasticity of the collisions of these balls with the floor or sidewalk compare with the elasticity of the collisions using the Superball?

Repeat the experiment with as many balls used in sports as you can find. You could try a baseball, a softball, a basketball, a golf ball,

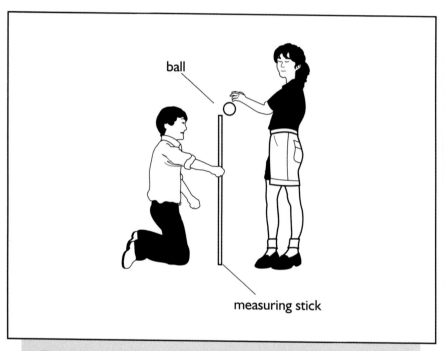

ball

measuring stick

Figure 19. To what height does the ball bounce after colliding with the floor?

a handball, a lacrosse ball, a soccer ball, a squash ball, a tennis ball, and so on. How many different balls used in sports did you try? For which of the balls you tested was the collision most elastic? Least elastic?

In all the experiments you tried, did you observe any totally elastic collisions? Did you observe any totally inelastic collisions?

Exploring on Your Own

Does the surface with which a ball collides affect the bounce height? To find out, try dropping the same balls on different surfaces. You might try wood, concrete, tile, brick, grass, dirt, and so on.

Can you find any relationship between the height to which a ball bounces and the number of previous bounces it has made after being dropped?

Watch the collision between an athlete who has jumped into the air and the ground with which she or he collides. How does the athlete cushion the collision?

4-4
Rules for Game Balls

According to the rules, a soccer ball must have a circumference (distance around) of 67–71 centimeters (27–28 inches), a weight of 397–454 grams (14–16 ounces), and be inflated to a pressure of 9.0 to 10.5 pounds per square inch (0.6–0.7 atmosphere, or 0.63–0.74 kilograms/square centimeter).

Find a soccer ball and use a tape measure to determine its circumference. Does the ball's circumference meet the requirements of the rule?

Use a balance to weigh the ball. How much does it weigh? Does the ball's weight meet the rule?

Using a pressure gauge, measure the air pressure inside the ball. What is the air pressure? Does it meet the rule?

In basketball, the rules require that the ball must have a certain "bounciness," or elasticity. As described in the rules of the game: *When dropped to the playing surface from a height of 6 feet, measured to the bottom of the ball, it should rebound to a height measured to the top of the ball of not less than 49 inches or more than 54 inches.*

Find a basketball. Then tape two yardsticks together and test the ball to see if it meets the bounciness rule described above. Repeat the experiment several times to make sure the results are nearly the same each time. How high does the ball bounce? Does the ball you tested have the bounciness required by the rules?

Does the surface on which the ball lands affect its bounce? To find out, try dropping the same ball on different surfaces. You might try wood, concrete, tile, macadam, and so on. What do you find?

As you have seen, a basketball must bounce to a height that lies between 5/9 and 5/8 of the height from which it is dropped. (Remember, a basketball is about 9 inches in diameter.) Is a regulation soccer ball as bouncy as a regulation basketball?

To find out, hold a soccer ball that meets the rules' requirements so that the bottom of the ball is level with the top of a yardstick or meterstick. Release the ball onto a wooden or tiled floor. Watch the bottom of the ball closely. How high does it rise after it hits the floor? Repeat the experiment several times to make sure the results are nearly the same each time. To what fraction of its original height does the ball rise? How does the bounciness of a regulation soccer ball compare with the bounciness of a regulation basketball?

To see how field conditions affect the bounciness of a soccer ball, repeat the bounciness test on parts of a field that are covered with: (a) tall, thick grass; (b) short, thick grass; (c) soft dirt; (d) hard-packed dirt; (e) mud. (If the field is dry, ask the owner's permission to soak a small area near the edge of the field with water to make it muddy.)

The valve used to inflate the ball can also be used to release most of the air from a regulation soccer ball. After some of the air has been released, repeat the test for bounciness. How does reducing the air pressure within the ball affect its bounciness? How does it affect the weight of the ball? Can you explain why it changes the weight?

Pump the ball back to its original pressure. Then add more air to the ball. How does increasing the pressure affect the bounciness of the ball?

4-5
Collisions: Hot and Cold

Some baseball teams in the past have been accused of heating or cooling baseballs before a game. Would the temperature of the balls make a difference? Some people claim that the elasticity of the materials inside a baseball increases with temperature. If this is true, a team with long-ball hitters might improve its chances

Things you will need:
- baseballs
- wooden floor
- yardstick or meterstick
- freezer
- an adult
- oven
- friend
- gloves

of winning by using livelier balls—balls that had been warmed before game time. On the other hand, a team that depends on defense, speed, and pitching would benefit from a less lively ball, so they might place game balls in the freezer prior to a contest.

To find out if temperature has any effect on the elasticity of baseballs, have a friend hold a yardstick or meterstick upright on a wooden floor. (A wooden floor is recommended because the bats used in professional baseball are made of wood.) Hold a baseball so that the bottom of the ball is level with the top of the yardstick or meterstick. Release the ball. Ask the friend holding the measuring stick to watch the bottom of the ball closely to see how high the ball bounces after it hits the floor.

Repeat the experiment several times to make sure the results are nearly the same each time. How high does the ball bounce? To what fraction of its original height does it rise?

Find several baseballs that all bounce to very nearly the same height after falling one yard or one meter. Place one or more of these balls in a freezer for several hours. **Ask an adult** to place one or more of the balls in a warm (150°F) oven for several hours.

Have your friend put on gloves to avoid injury in handling the hot and cold baseballs. Then, as you did before, measure the bounce heights of the warm and cold baseballs. What do you find? What effect could heating or cooling baseballs have on the game?

Adjusting the temperature of baseballs is illegal. To avoid any such action, all game balls are now in the control of the umpire several hours before a game. Do you agree that changing the temperature of game balls should be illegal? Why?

4-6*
A Model for Collisions and Protection from Collisions

One way to investigate collisions is to make models of them. The same approach can be used in examining techniques for protecting people from injuries resulting from collisions. Experiments can be carried out using the models.

In this experiment, you will use a lump of clay to represent

Things you will need:

- lump of clay about the size of a baseball

- a hard surface such as a concrete wall

- an old bedsheet or a similar piece of cloth

- clothesline

- clothespins

the head of any athlete who wears a helmet, such as a cyclist, football player, hockey player, and so on. Begin by rolling a large lump of modeling clay into a ball. Throw the ball of clay against a hard surface such as a concrete wall. The wall will apply a force to the clay and bring it to rest. What is the shape of the clay after it hits the wall? How is the shape of the ball of clay affected by the speed with which you threw it? Was this collision elastic, inelastic, or partially elastic?

Next, you need a model of a protective device—a device that will lengthen the time of the impulse needed to bring the clay to rest. You can use an old bedsheet or any other similar piece of cloth. Hang the sheet from a clothesline. The sheet can represent the suspension and cushions inside a football helmet or hockey helmet.

Re-form the clay into a ball and throw it against the sheet at about the fastest speed it had when you threw it against the wall. The ball again comes to rest. How does the shape of the clay ball after this collision compare with its shape after it hit the hard wall? Explain how the model of a helmet affected the damage to the "head" due to the collision.

Exploring on Your Own

Design, build, and test your own model for collisions and protective devices to prevent injuries caused by collisions. **Do not try them out on yourself.** Use them only with models.

Design, build, and test a model of a protective system for race-car drivers.

4-7*
Protection from Collisions: Another Model

Things you will need:

- uncooked eggs

- firm, hard surface, such as a floor or sidewalk

- various materials, such as cotton, newspapers, small boxes, tape, rubber bands, elastic bands, etc.

- yardstick or meterstick

Collisions between players are part of the game in hockey and football, but they occur in other sports as well. Baseball players are told to call for a fly ball by yelling, "I got it! I got it!" The reason for the call is to prevent collisions between fielders. An infielder calling for the ball is supposed to give way if he hears an outfielder calling for the ball. Why do you think the outfielder is the preferred player? Despite their calls, baseball players do sometimes collide, and sometimes are injured as a result.

Player collisions are also common in basketball, soccer, lacrosse, even doubles tennis. Despite the danger, football was originally played without helmets, and professional hockey players, even goalies, were not required to wear helmets for many years. Today's players are better protected because they do wear helmets and other protective equipment. But how do helmets reduce head injuries?

Your brain is surrounded by a bony skull that protects it. A thin layer of fluid between the brain and the skull serves as padding so that the brain will not slam against the hard skull. In this experiment, you will use an egg to represent the human head. The egg's shell corresponds to the skull; the fluid inside the egg represents the brain.

Your task is to design and build a "helmet" for the egg so that it will not break when it falls to the floor or ground from a height of 2 meters (about 6 feet). After designing the "helmet," gather the materials you need and build a helmet to fit the egg.

Once you have built the helmet, test it by dropping it and the egg within it from a height of 2 meters onto a hard surface. If the egg does not break, you have designed a good helmet.

You might organize a contest to see who can build the best helmet for an egg. For those whose eggs survive a 2-meter fall, **ask an adult to help you** extend the test to 3 meters or higher. What do you find are the key factors in building a good helmet? What scientific principles related to impulse (force x time) are involved in designing and building a satisfactory protective helmet?

Exploring on Your Own

Examine the protective equipment worn by football players, such as helmets, shoulder pads, rib pads, thigh pads, and so on. How do they reduce injuries caused by collisions between players, and between players and the surface on which the game is played? How are these pieces of protective equipment related to the scientific principles of momentum and impulse?

What common injuries related to football and other sports are not reduced by protective equipment? How might these types of injuries be diminished?

4-8
Collisions and Mass: Another Model

Thousands of experiments have shown that momentum is conserved (does not change); that is, the product of the mass and velocity of colliding objects at the beginning of a collision is the same as it is after the collision. Of course, the earth is often involved

in collisions, so it may appear that momentum is not conserved. For example, if you are at rest, your momentum is zero. If you start to run, your momentum increases. But if momentum is conserved, how can there be momentum when the original momentum was zero?

The answer is that in order to move forward you had to push backward with your feet against the earth (Newton's second law). The earth pushed forward on you (Newton's third law) with an equal but opposite force for the same length of time that you pushed on it. The impulse applied to you and to the earth were equal but opposite in direction. As a result, your momentum and the earth's momentum are equal but in opposite directions. The total momentum is still zero. Two vectors representing these two momentums would be equal but opposite. Their sum would be zero. So momentum was conserved.

From what you know about force, momentum, and impulse, why do you think football coaches like their players to be big as well as fast? In a sport where collisions are part of the game, is there any scientific reason for preferring big players? You can find out by using steel balls to represent football players and watching what happens when they collide.

Place a grooved ruler on a level table or countertop. Place two identical steel balls in the groove of the ruler, as shown in Figure 20. The groove will keep the balls in a line.

Put one ball near the center of the ruler and an identical ball at one end of the ruler. Give the ball at the end a push so that it rolls and collides with the other ball. What happens after they collide? Which ball is at rest? Which ball is moving?

Repeat the experiment, but this time place a heavy ball at the middle of the ruler and a lighter ball at the end. What happens when the lighter ball rolls into the heavier one?

Now place the lighter ball at the center of the ruler and the heavy ball at the end. What happens when the heavy ball rolls into the light one?

When a light body that is moving hits one with the same mass, the one that was moving stops (or almost stops) and the one that was at rest moves away with (or nearly with) the speed that the first body had. When a light body hits a heavy one, the light one bounces back and the heavy one moves forward with less speed than the light

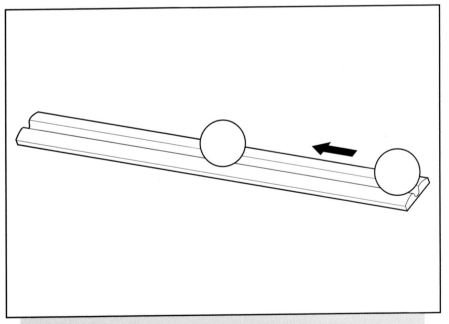

Figure 20. Steel balls on a grooved ruler can be used to model collisions.

object had. When a heavy ball hits a light object, they both continue to move forward, as when a fullback bowls over the safety who is tackling him. How are these collisions like those found on a football field? How are they different?

Of course, the model used here is not perfect. The collisions between steel balls are elastic; that is, they are very bouncy; it is like a collision between springs. In the next experiment, you will use a less elastic model.

4-9
Collisions and Mass: A Less Elastic Model

Things you will need:

• 2 identical toy cars or trucks (about 15 cm [6 inches] long)

• modeling clay

• friend

In the last experiment, you used steel balls to represent colliding football players. In this experiment, you will use toy trucks and clay. These collisions will be less elastic (springy) than those with steel balls. They will be more like collisions involving good tackling, in which the players stick together as a collision is made. From what you know about momentum and the conservation of momentum, try to predict the outcome of each collision before you try it.

Put big lumps of clay on the front bumpers of two toy cars or trucks. Ask a friend to help you. Before you make the two vehicles collide, practice pushing them so that you and your friend can make them move at very nearly the same speed. Now make the trucks collide when each truck is moving toward the other at moderate and equal speed. The trucks should meet head-on as the lumps of clay on the bumpers bang into one another. What happens to the trucks after this collision between bodies of equal mass and speed? Were you able to predict the result?

Next, make the trucks collide head-on while one is moving very slowly and the other is moving at moderate speed. What happens when objects of equal mass moving at different speeds collide?

Now have one truck moving at moderate speed collide with an identical truck that is at rest. What happens? Are the results as you predicted?

Make one truck or car heavier than the other by sticking lots of clay in it or on it. Let the trucks collide head-on at equal speeds. What happens when the heavy car meets the lighter car moving at the same speed in the opposite direction?

Let a light vehicle at rest be struck head-on by a heavier vehicle that is moving. Finally, watch a collision in which a heavy vehicle at rest is hit by a lighter vehicle that is moving. What happens in each of these collisions? Were you able to predict the results of these collisions correctly?

Based on what you have observed in this experiment, why do football coaches like to have players who are both fast and heavy?

5

Playing the Angles and Distances

Billiards is not the only game in which playing the angles is important. Every sport involves angles. Sometimes it is the angle from which one has to shoot a ball or a puck toward a goal. It may be the angle from which a throw must be made, or the best angle for a tackler to pursue a runner.

Distances are important, too. Basketball, soccer, hockey, and lacrosse players like to be as close to the goal as possible when they shoot. But defenders try to make them shoot from greater distances and from difficult angles. From what distance or angle is it impractical to try to shoot for a goal? The experiments in this chapter will help you answer this question.

5-1*
Shooting Soccer Balls from Different Angles

Generally, the percentage of successful shots in soccer are related to the angle from which the shot is made. As you will find in doing this experiment, the width of the open goal that is visible decreases as the angle increases. What effect does angle have on shooting success? This experiment will help you to find out.

Things you will need:

• soccer ball

• soccer field and goal

• tape measure

• pail

• 2 friends

• notebook

• pen or pencil

• powder or sticks

A soccer goal is 8 yards wide, but you seldom see the entire goal open. To make the shooting more realistic, place a pail 2 yards from one goal post, as shown in Figure 21. Then measure out the shooting positions for different angles, as shown in Table 1. Stand at those numbered positions, as shown in Figure 21, and take shots at the two-yard opening between the goal post and the pail. The angle between the center of the open goal line and the point where the shot is made is indicated in Table 1. The positions are all 15 yards (45 ft) from the center of the two-foot-wide goal. To find the positions for each angle, begin by marking a line perpendicular to the center of the two-foot-wide goal. All positions will be measured along this line and then along lines perpendicular to this line as shown on Figure 21 and as indicated in Table 1.

Use powder or sticks to mark the positions for the various angle shots on the field. Then take about five or six shots from each position. Have a friend record the shots taken and made from each angle. Another friend can return the ball to you.

Then let your friends try the same experiment while you record results or return shots.

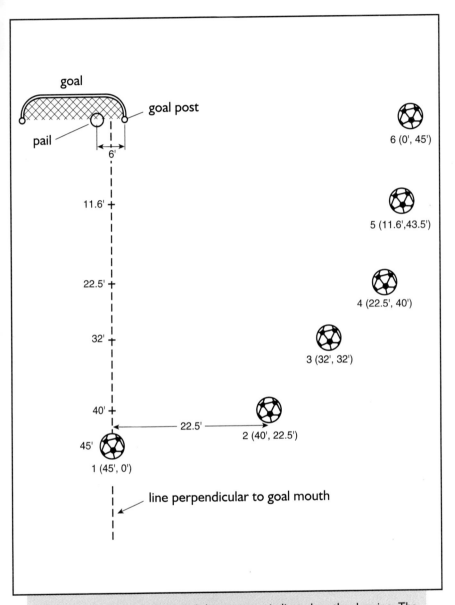

Figure 21. Position numbers and distances are indicated on the drawing. The numbers in parentheses are, first, the distance along a line perpendicular to the goal mouth, followed by the distance to the right of that line. All shooting positions are 45 feet from the goal mouth. Similar positions can be established on the other side of the line perpendicular to the goal.

Table 1: How to set up positions for angle shots.

Position Number	To establish a shooting angle of	Measure a distance along a line perpendicular to the mouth of the goal that is	Then measure a distance perpendicular to the first line that has a length of
1	0°	45.0 ft	0
2	30°	40.0 ft	22.5 ft
3	45°	32.0 ft	32.0 ft
4	60°	22.5 ft	40.0 ft
5	75°	11.6 ft (11' 7")	43.5 ft
6	90°	0	45.0 ft

What is your percentage of success from each of the angles where you took shots?

What happens to the percentage of shots made as the angle to the mouth of the goal increases?

Is there any way to kick a goal when the angle is 90 degrees and no part of the open goal can be seen?

Exploring on Your Own

Design and carry out an experiment to find out how distance from the goal affects the percentage of shots made. Should there be an active goalie while you conduct this experiment?

5-2*
Shooting Angles in Hockey

As in soccer, hockey players seldom see the entire width of the goal because they have to shoot from positions that are to the left or right of the goal. What effect does angle have on shooting success? This experiment will help you to find out how the shooting angle in hockey affects the percentage of shots made.

Use a few drops of paint to mark various positions on the

Things you will need:

- hockey rink with goals
- hockey stick
- several pucks
- paint
- 2 friends
- notebook
- pen or pencil
- tape measure
- 2 blankets

ice, such as those shown in Figure 22. As you can see, the angle to the goal mouth increases as you move from center (C) to the left (L) or to the right (R). The distances should all be the same. In the diagram, the distances in parentheses give the distances to measure to obtain a constant distance of 15 feet (15') from the center of the net. The first number gives the number of feet to measure from the goal mouth outward along a line perpendicular to the goal mouth. The second number gives the number of feet to measure to the right or left of the first measurement. For example, for a 30-degree angle, measure out 13 feet (13' from the goal) and then 7.5 feet (7.5') to the left or right from the 13' measurement.

To be sure all the distances are the same, use a tape measure to find the distance from the center of the goal mouth to the point from which you will shoot. To make the shooting a little more challenging, hang blankets over the mouth of the goal so that only half of it is open.

Take several shots at the open net from each position you have marked. Have a friend record the shots taken and made for each angle. A second friend can retrieve the pucks. Then let your

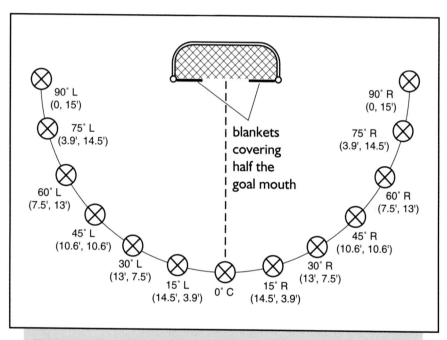

Figure 22. Try shooting pucks from different angles to the goal. Possible positions are shown by the circled X's. How does shooting angle affect the percentage of shots that are successful?

friends try the same experiment while you record results or return pucks.

What is the percentage of success from each of the angles where shots were taken? What happens to the percentage of shots that enter the goal as the angle to the mouth of the goal increases?

Exploring on Your Own

Design and carry out an experiment to find out how distance from the goal affects the percentage of shots made.

Design and carry out an experiment to see how the impulse that a goalie must apply to a puck to prevent it from entering the goal is related to the angle from which it is shot.

5-3

How a Hockey Goalie Reduces the Shooting Angle

Hockey goalies are told to cut down an offensive player's shooting angle by moving toward the opponent. In this experiment, you will see what that means.

Things you will need:

- hockey rink with goals
- friend
- blanket
- paper or pencil
- ruler

Ask a friend to hold a blanket, folded so it is about half as wide as the hockey goal, in front of the goal. The blanket represents the area taken up by a goalie.

Stand about 15 feet in front of the goal. How much of the goal is open—that is, how much of the goal is not covered by the blanket that represents the goalie?

Now have your friend move slowly toward you while holding the blanket as before. What happens to the amount of open goal that you can see as your friend moves closer to you? How far does your friend have to move toward you before none of the goal mouth is open to your view?

Next, move to a point where you are still 15 feet from the goal but to one side of it. Repeat the experiment. How much of the goal can you see this time when your friend holds the blanket and turns toward you? How far does your friend have to move toward you before none of the goal mouth is open to your view?

Finally, move to a point where you are still 15 feet from the goal but even farther to the side of it. Repeat the experiment. How much of the goal can you see this time when your friend holds the blanket and turns toward you? How far does your friend have to move toward you before none of the goal mouth is open to your view?

What risk does a goalie take when he or she moves out to cut down an opponent's shooting angle?

From the results of the experiment, what can you say happens to an offensive player's shooting angle when a goalie closes down on him or her? What distance does a goalie need to move out from the goal to eliminate any open net visible to a shooter when the shooter is far to one side of the goal?

Make a diagram based on this experiment to show how shooting angles are reduced when a goalie moves out toward the shooter.

5-4
Basketball and Shooting Angles

What is the best angle for making basketball shots from the floor? This experiment will help you to find out.

Stand a few feet from the basket and try taking shots at various angles—"line drives," 40–50-degree arches, and "rainbows" (see Figure 23).

Things you will need:
• basketball
• basketball court
• paper or pencil
• ruler

Which launching angle seems to give you the greatest shooting success?

Careful analysis shows that shots made at angles close to 49 degrees are most likely to be successful. Players with good control of the speed of their shots can make low angle shots, but the range of speeds for such angles is quite low. Draw a diagram to show why the ball, which has a 9.5-inch diameter, is more likely to enter the 18-inch basket at some angles and less likely at other angles.

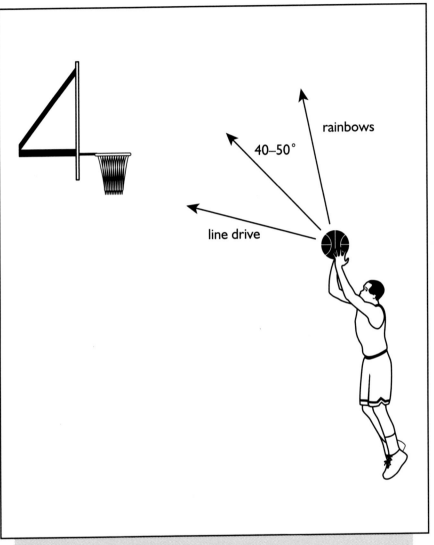

Figure 23. What is the best angle at which to launch a basketball in order to make the shot?

5-5*
Basketball and Shooting Distances

What effect does distance have on shooting success? This experiment will help you find out.

Things you will need:

- basketball
- basketball court
- yardstick, meterstick, or tape measure
- 2 friends
- pen or pencil
- notebook

Take a basketball and try to make some shots from both sides of the court at various distances as measured from a point directly under the basket. Take at least several shots from each position. Have one friend record the distance, the number of shots taken, and the number made. A second friend can retrieve your shots and return the ball to you.

After you have taken some shots, let your friends try the same experiment while you record results or return shots. In that way, none of you will become tired, and your results will be more reliable. If you do tire and feel you are not doing as well as you could, spread the experiment over several days.

What is your percentage of success from each of the positions where you took shots? What happens to the percentage of shots made as you move farther from the basket?

If you were able to make shots from beyond the three-point line, what is your shooting percentage from there compared with your percentage from inside the line?

Is there one particular distance or place where you found your shooting success to be the greatest?

Make a diagram to show how a small aiming error, that might still result in a successful shot if made close to the basket, will be a miss at a large distance.

On the basis of your results, do you agree that a player may often find his or her "spot"—a position on the floor where the player enjoys the greatest shooting success?

Exploring on Your Own

Design an experiment to see how the angle on the court, as measured from a line extending down the middle of the court, affects shooting percentage. Can a player shoot as successfully from the side of the court as from a point in front of the basket if the distances are the same?

5-6*
Lefties and the Distance to First Base

Only 11 percent of all people are left-handed, yet more than half the major-league batting titles have been won by left-handed batters. Is there some advantage to batting left-handed? This experiment will help you find out.

Things you will need:
- baseball field or 90-foot length on a lawn or park
- cardboard (if necessary)
- baseball bat
- stopwatch or watch with a second hand or mode
- several friends

Find a baseball field or mark off a distance of 90 feet on a lawn or in a park. If you mark off a 90-foot distance, use two pieces of cardboard to represent home plate and first base.

Stand at home plate holding a bat as a left-handed batter. Have a friend with a watch shout, "Go!" When you hear "Go," swing the bat at an imaginary pitch, drop the bat, and run as fast as you can to first base.

Have your friend record the number of seconds it took you to swing the bat and run to first base.

After resting for several minutes, repeat the experiment, but this time stand at the plate as a right-handed batter.

Have a number of different people do the same experiment. For every person, record the time it takes him or her to swing and run to first base from each side of home plate.

For each person who carries out the experiment, compare the times required to reach first base as a left-handed and as a right-handed batter. What can you conclude? What advantage do left-handed batters have in reaching first base?

What percentage of major-league pitchers are right-handed? What additional advantage do left-handed batters have? Why do you think left-handed batters are more likely to win major-league batting titles, despite the fact that only one in nine people is left-handed?

Exploring on Your Own

Why are there no left-handed catchers in major-league baseball?

Why are there no left-handed shortstops, third basemen, or second basemen in major-league baseball? Is there any advantage to being a left-handed first baseman?

Do left-handed athletes have an advantage in sports other than baseball?

Are left-handed people also left-footed?

Most people have a dominant eye just as they have a dominant hand. To find out which eye is your dominant one, align your thumb with some distant object. Now close first one eye and then the other. The eye that still aligns with your thumb is your dominant eye. Test a number of people to see which eye is dominant.

What advantage would a left-handed batter have if he or she had a dominant right eye? What advantage would a right-handed batter have if he or she had a dominant left eye?

Test a number of (both left- and right-handed) good and mediocre hitters for eye dominance. (Of course, you should not tell them what you consider their batting skill to be.) Do you find any evidence that a right-handed batter with a dominant left eye or a left-handed batter with a dominant right eye has a better batting average?

List of Suppliers

The following companies supply the materials that may be needed for science fair projects:

Carolina Biological Supply Co.
2700 York Road
Burlington, NC 27215
(800) 334-5551
http://www.carolina.com

Central Scientific Co. (CENCO)
3300 Cenco Parkway
Franklin Park, IL 60131
(800) 262-3626
http://www.cenconet.com

Connecticut Valley Biological Supply Co., Inc.
82 Valley Road, Box 326
Southampton, MA 01073
(800) 628-7748

Delta Education
P.O. Box 915
Hudson, NH 03051-0915
(800) 258-1302

Edmund Scientific Co.
101 East Gloucester Pike
Barrington, NJ 08007
(609) 547-3488

Fisher Science Education
485 S. Frontage Road
Burr Ridge, IL 60521
(800) 955-1177
http://www.fisheredu.com/

Frey Scientific
100 Paragon Parkway
Mansfield, OH 44905
(800) 225-3739

Nasco-Fort Atkinson
P.O. Box 901
Fort Atkinson, WI 53538-0901
(800) 558-9595

Nasco-Modesto
P.O. Box 3837
Modesto, CA 95352-3837
(800) 558-9595
http://www.nasco.com

Sargent-Welch/VWR Scientific
P.O. Box 5229
Buffalo Grove, IL 60089-5229
(800) SAR-GENT
http://www.SargentWelch.com

Science Kit & Boreal
Laboratories
777 East Park Drive
Tonawanda, NY 14150
(800) 828-7777
http://sciencekit.com

Ward's Natural Science Establishment, Inc.
P.O. Box 92912
Rochester, NY 14692-9012
(800) 962-2660
http://www.wardsci.com

Further Reading

Adair, Robert K. *The Physics of Baseball*. New York: Harper and Row, 1990.

Adams, Richard, and Robert Gardner. *Ideas for Science Projects*, Revised Edition. Danbury, Conn.: Franklin Watts, 1997.

———. *More Ideas for Science Projects*, Revised Edition. Danbury, Conn.: Franklin Watts, 1998.

Barr, George. *Sports Science for Young People*. New York: Dover, 1990.

Bochinski, Julianne Blair. *The Complete Handbook of Science Fair Projects*. New York: John Wiley, 1996.

Brancazio, Peter J. *Sport Science*. New York: Simon and Schuster, 1985.

Gardner, Robert. *Science and Sports*. New York: Franklin Watts, 1988.

———. *Science Fair Projects—Planning, Presenting, Succeeding*. Springfield, N.J.: Enslow Publishers, Inc., 1999.

Isberg, Emily. *Performance: Sports, Science, and the Body in Action*. New York: Simon & Schuster Books for Young Readers, 1989.

Kettlecamp, Larry. *Modern Sports Science*. New York: William Morrow, 1986.

Krieger, Melanie Jacobs. *How to Excel in Science Competitions, Revised and Updated*. Springfield, N.J.: Enslow Publishers, Inc., 1999.

Markle, Sandra. *The Young Scientist's Guide to Successful Science Projects*. New York: Lothrop, Lee, and Shepard, 1990.

The Ontario Science Centre. *Sportworks: More than 50 Fun Activities that Explore the Science of Sport*. Reading, Mass.: Addison Wesley, 1989.

Schrier, Eric, and William F. Allman, eds., *Newton at the Bat: The Science in Sports*. New York: Scribner, 1984.

Tocci, Salvatore. *How to Do a Science Fair Project*, Revised Edition. Danbury, Conn.: Franklin Watts, 1997.

Internet Addresses

Bicycle Helmet Safety Institute. *Bicycle Helmet Safety Institute.* June 7, 1999. <http://www.bhsi.org/> (June 7, 1999).

The Exploratorium. *Sport! Science @ The Exploratorium*. 1998. <http://www.exploratorium.edu/sports/index.html> (June 7, 1999).

Franklin Institute Science Museum. 1995–1999. <http://sln.fi.edu/> (June 7, 1999).

Morano, David. *Experimental Science Projects: An Introductory Level Guide*. May 27, 1995. <http://www.isd77.k12.mn.us/resources/cf/SciProjIntro.html> (June 7, 1999).

Washington State University. "Ask a Scientist." *The MAD Scientist Network*. August 18, 1998. <http://www.madsci.org> (June 7, 1999).

Index

A
acceleration, 42
accelerometer, 51, 53
air pressure, 57
angles of shots
  basketball, 116
  football, 28–29
  hockey, 111, 113–115
  soccer, 108, 110

B
baseball, 12–13, 16–17, 75,
  86–87, 96–97
baseball bat, 72, 74
basketball, 18–19, 35–36, 80,
  94–95, 116
biking, 53
bounce, 91, 93–95

C
center of gravity, 59–60, 63
  baseball bat, 72, 74
  football, 68–69, 71
  human body, 64–65
  and sports, 66–67
centripetal force, 51, 53
circular motion, 51, 53–54
collisions
  between balls and
    surfaces, 91, 93
  elastic and inelastic,
    90–91, 93, 104
  models, 98–106
  models for protective
    equipment, 98–101

sports, 89–91, 93, 100
and temperature, 96–97

D
distance, 118, 120

E
energy
  elastic, 89–91, 93
  transformations, 89

F
first law of motion, 33–34, 39
  basketball, 35–36
  hockey, 37
follow-through, 83–84
football, 27, 68–69, 71, 84
forces perpendicular to motion,
  48, 50, 51, 53–54
friction, 33, 41, 48, 51
  and cleats, 76
  and spin, 78, 80

G
Galileo, 36
gravity, 55

H
hockey, 19–20, 21, 24, 37, 83,
  88–89, 111, 113–115

I
impulse, 81–82, 85, 102
  and catching, 86–89
  and collisions, 89–91, 93